AF674579

THE BASIS FOR ARTISTIC AND INDUSTRIAL REVIVAL IN INDIA

The Basis for Artistic and Industrial Revival in India

E.B. HAVELL

MANOHAR
2025

First published 1991
Reprinted 2025
First eBook edition 2025

© Manohar Publishers & Distributors, 2025

All rights reserved. No part of this publication may be reproduced or transmitted, in any form or by any means, without prior permission of the publisher.

ISBN 978-93-6080-523-4 (Hb)
ISBN 978-93-6080-597-5 (ebook)

Published by
Ajay Kumar Jain *for*
Manohar Publishers & Distributors
4753/23 Ansari Road, Daryaganj
New Delhi 110 002

Printed and bound in India

PREFACE

IN the following pages, originally written in a series of letters to *The Hinḍū* of Madras, I have endeavoured to set down in a form intelligible to expert and non-expert the results of twenty years' practical experience in all teaching in India, hoping that they may be useful in promoting the cause I have at heart—the revival of Indian art and craft.

As Lord Minto declared recently, the most pressing questions of the moment in India are educational, sociological and industrial. All three are closely involved in the future of Indian art and craft, the preservation of which is not only vital to India but is a matter of international importance; for the possibility of building upon the basis of Indian civilisation and culture, a better social and industrial system than that which now exists in Europe is a matter which concerns all nations. In Great Britain national art education is a problem of which a satisfactory solution has yet to be found. In India, where the difficulties should be infinitely less, as the opportunities are so much greater, it can hardly be said with truth that it has ever received serious consideration from the Indian point of view.

E. B. HAVELL

LONDON
February, 1912

CONTENTS

CHAPTER I

THE THEORY OF ART

BEFORE entering upon practical details, I want to make clear my position on the theory of art, and I would ask my readers always to keep this clearly in mind. In the present age, artistic principles are often confused by the use of worn out shibboleths, and artistic practice falsified by the application of empiric prescriptions. Nowhere does art suffer more from charlatanism than in India. Let me give some illustrations of false art. There is no respect for art in the millionaire who invests his surplus wealth in pictures and the costliest furniture so that his taste may be admired, or his wealth envied, by his poorer brethren. There is none in the man who decorates his house in a style archæologically correct, or dresses himself in the latest foreign fashion, so that he may be considered 'up-to-date' by his fellows. There is none in the engineer who having made some hideous construction seeks to beautify it by covering it with meaningless ornament. But there is true art instinct in the humble peasant who takes the choicest flowers he can find and with patience and skill weaves them into a garland for the village shrine. And so there is in the craftsman or labourer who, rejoicing in the cunning of his hand and with no thought of extra profit for himself, puts into his work the best that his knowledge and skill can produce.

Art is not meant to be a speciality reserved for the enjoyment of the rich, nor is its scope restricted to the special walks in life to which the artist and art workman devote themselves. Neither are the perception and realisation of art only intended, as is so often supposed, to add to the pleasures of life. This is the mistaken idea of the ascetic, or puritan, who condemns music and the higher forms of artistic effort, as an unworthy indulgence of the senses. Art, properly employed, is, as the great Akbar said, an aid to the understanding of the divine nature; its proper use is to fulfil the divine purpose in the intellectual and spiritual evolution of the perfect human state. Every faculty and every sense may be put to immoral uses. The artistic faculty is often abused; therefore it is important to understand the right use of art, not to stand aloof from it and regard it as irreligious.

Another equally mistaken notion is that which regards the artistic faculty as a peculiar one which is outside the scope of general education. So far from this being the case, it is the essential quality which distinguishes good education, from bad. Art is a universal faculty. It is the ideal, or creative sense, which leads to the highest achievements in every walk of life. If this higher faculty is neglected, as is often the case in modern bookish education, the so-called educated man tends to become an intellectual automaton which can only record the mental impressions of school and university life, and is quite incapable of helping forward humanity by adding to the sum of human knowledge and experience, as every educated man should do.

It is because the Anglo-Indian educational system has no ideal, beyond that of imparting to Indian students the intellectual impressions of Oxford, Cambridge, Aberdeen and London, that it has failed to stimulate a real intellectual life in Indian Universities. I think, therefore, that the Government would be well-advised to encourage to the utmost the movement for a national scheme of education which has been lately started in Bengal; but the leaders of this movement, in taking this great responsibility upon their shoulders, should beware lest they fall into the same pit as those who have directed the official system for the last fifty years. They may hold up a higher ideal in endeavouring to create an educational system more closely related to Indian life than that of modern Indian Universities, but in the understanding of the educational uses of art, and in the appreciation of the vast importance for India of keeping alive its old artistic traditions, I have not noticed that this embryonic scheme of national education as yet shows signs of being superior to the Anglo-Indian one.

Art in relation to industry, or the practical concerns of life, is the influence which ennobles human labour and helps us to realise the identity of the laws of man's living with those of the universal life. For, the harmony which art, justly applied, brings into human life, is truly an echo of that eternal harmony which sustains the universe. Reduced to abstract terms, art applied to industrial purposes may be represented by the triple combination or formula, Fitness—Beauty, or Rhythm—Love, or Worship. Fitness for the use to which a thing is to be applied; Beauty growing spontaneously from the perfect fitness (for man does not live by bread alone); Love, the source of highest inspiration, proceeding from the understanding of the identity of a perfect life with the perfect harmony of divine laws.

In every age and every part of the world, when the progress of national development has reached its highest point, intellectually and spiritually, art combines all three qualities and the absence of any one of them is a symptom of the degradation of art and of national character. An art which is produced entirely by machinery, as much of the art of the present day is produced, must obviously lack the quality of love, which no machine can feel; and art thereby becomes a sham and make-believe. But even in an age of great artistic achievement, like that of the Italian Renaissance, one can detect the signs of coming degeneration in the divorce of art from utility and from religion. Then art was produced, not for love and worship, but to gratify a passion for show and pleasure. The decadence quickly followed, and European art has hardly yet begun to regain its ennobling influence on national life. The splendid art of the Mogul period in India is a parallel instance. The high purpose of art was then also debased for the pleasure and distraction of the Court. There is love and beauty to be found in that art, but not the universal love; only a selfish and personal kind of love. Here is one of the chief clues to the degeneration which is visible in modern Indian art.

An art which is truly great strikes deep down into national life, and permeates the whole national character. It does not appear only at Court shows and festivals. Art has its real beginnings in elemental ideas of cleanliness, decency, and order. It is only in a corrupt and effete state of society that artistic ideas are associated with dilapidation, dirt and inutility. If social reformers in India would realise this, they would understand that their best hopes lie in a true renaissance of art in India, for the highest art is the art of good living.

CHAPTER II

PRESENT CONDITIONS OF ART IN INDIA AND REASONS FOR DEGENERATION

It may, perhaps, be considered inconsistent of one, who like myself is continually bewailing the decay of Indian art, to say that conditions for an artistic revival are much more favourable in India than they are in Europe. It is true that in India there are no Royal Academies, few Schools of Art and Museums, and that art is more or less ignored in the whole educational system. But it is equally true that art in India has even now a much greater hold upon national life than it has in England, and that those conditions which all serious art and social reformers in Europe are now trying to revive—conditions which had always existed in every great art epoch in the West as well as in the East—are still surviving in India to a much larger extent than they are in any European country at the present time. These are conditions which make art a part of life and work, not merely an amusement and a luxury; and without such conditions, art may justly be regarded with indifference by all who have to deal with the serious affairs of life.

It is not true that because in Europe many wonderful inventions of machinery (and many very foolish ones) have been made, that these conditions have been fundamentally altered, that art is revolutionised and has to surrender to the dictates of modern scientific ideas. But it is just as foolish for the artist to ignore modern science as it is for the scientist to ignore Indian art. All knowledge is given to man for its proper use, and there is no antagonism between real science and real art. Dr. Coomaraswamy says:

> The machine has come to stay and, rightly used, may be transformed from a curse into a blessing. The problem is not how to abolish machinery, but how so to regulate it that it shall serve without enslaving man; how to stop competition between machine and hand-work, by defining and delimiting intelligently the proper spheres of each. The community cannot afford to dispense with the intellectual and imaginative forces, the educational and ethical factors, which go with the existence of skilled craftsmen and small workshops.

The greatest mistake that Anglo-Indian administrators have made is in ignoring these educational and ethical factors. If the sole duty of the Indian Government in relation to art and industry lies in the ideal put forward by Professor Lees Smith, the commercial expert—to make India take its place among the great industrial nations of the world—then there would be nothing wrong in ignoring, as Anglo-Indian administrators have always ignored, the educational and ethical factors represented by the existence of ten million Indian hereditary craftsmen. It is doubtless the easier way for Indians to throw aside all their artistic traditions as obsolete, to accept blindly the teaching of European commercial experts, to multiply factories and to join in the mad scramble for markets which Europe calls civilisation. But is this the ideal which will satisfy the Swaḍeshi reformer who is proud of India's past traditions, and of the intellectual and spiritual heritage which has been bequeathed to him? Is it the ideal of the nationalist who aims at achieving India's political freedom? Will India be freer, happier and wiser when, instead of lacs of village craftsmen, it has crores of mill-owners, mill-hands and shopkeepers, when the sound of the Swaḍeshi gramophons is heard in every village, when every town has its Swaḍeshi cotton-mills and shoddy-mills and also the Swaḍeshi music-halls and gin-palaces which are the inevitable accompaniments of these symbols of civilisation among the great industrial nations of Europe? If this be their Ideal, then Heaven save India from Swaḍeshi reformers!

You may say that this is not your ideal; but that, in present circumstances, it is necessary to compromise; that India is a poor country, and we must find the shortest and quickest way to provide subsistence for its poverty-stricken population—that is precisely the attitude of the Anglo-Indian who can only appreciate art in terms of rupees, annas and pies; not for an Indian who calls himself a Swaḍeshi reformer. It is an utterly false and insincere position. You cannot serve two masters—you must choose between God and Mammon. I do not mean by this that India is doomed to remain poverty-stricken while Europe waxes fatter and more prosperous, that her people must renounce all prospects of worldly wealth for the intellectual and spiritual life, but that the only sure way to national prosperity lies in clinging always to the highest intellectual and moral ideals. No nation has ever grown to greatness by compromising. India has sunk in the scale of nations because she has been false to her highest ideals, and India will only rise again when she holds up for herself and for humanity higher ones than modern Europe now brings her.

Those Swaḍeshi reformers who welcome the spread of European commercialism in India as a sign of India's coming regeneration, must be completely blind to its ultimate effects. Nowhere in India—not even in the direst time of famine and pestilence—is there such utter depravity, such hopeless physical, moral and spiritual degradation as that which exists in the great commercial cities of Europe, and directly brought about by modern industrial methods. When one takes into account the life of those who are only struggling to become rich, and the misery caused by the methods of modern commercialism, it is folly to suppose that India will find the remedy for her present suffering in becoming a competitor with western nations for the markets of the world. India can and no doubt will eventually regain her place among the great industrial nations, but if Swaḍeshi reformers wish to spare her industrial population the cruel experience of the nineteenth century in Europe, they must evolve a better system than that which many of them are attempting now to reproduce.

All the efforts of artistic and industrial reformers in Europe have been for many years directed towards the working out of a better system than that which is so foolishly held up as a pattern for India to follow. The results have not hitherto been so striking as to compel the attention of the man in the street, but nevertheless they afford the best object lesson for the Swaḍeshi reformer which European art and science can give him. It cannot be too often impressed upon Indian reformers, whose experience of Europe dates from thirty or forty years ago, that what we call progress in Europe now is something quite different to the ideas prevalent at that time. Anyone who attempts to follow the more recent developments of art and industry in Europe cannot fail to be impressed by the fact that the very methods which scientific and technical experts in India so often condemn as obsolete and useless, are just the methods to which the greatest attention is devoted here. Europe, in fact, has been for years deeply engaged in exploiting the knowledge of Indian handicraftsmen for the benefit of her own industries, while Indian industrial reformers as well as Anglo-Indian administrators can only think of importing from Europe those mechanical processes which kill all art in industry.

I will give an example which will apply particularly to the Madras Presidency, for it relates to an industry which was formerly a very great one there. Some years ago I had an official correspondence with some industrial experts in Holland who desired information regarding the Indian processes of dye-painting on silk and cotton cloth, analogous to those which are still practised by the native art workmen in the Dutch colony of Java. Subsequently, I learnt that a Dutch expert was sent out to India and Java to collect information on the spot. Recently, while on a visit to Holland, I observed the results of all this activity in the development of a new Dutch industry at Haarlem and elsewhere: very artistic hand-painted handkerchiefs, neckties, screen-cloths, etc., were being made by the old Indian and Javanese processes, which were followed in every detail—even the apparatus for the waxing process had been imported from Java. Later on, I discovered that the same processes were being adopted in technical schools in Germany and Italy. But in London I have been told by a well-known Madrasi merchant that he was quite unable to get what he wanted, Masulipatam hand-dyed cloths made by exactly the same processes, to meet the demand in Europe. He could easily take, he told me, Rs. 20,000 worth more, annually, if the workmen would only improve—*not their process—but the artistic quality of their work,* which had so much degenerated in the last fifty years.

Now I have often heard scientific experts in India, who believe themselves very much up-to-date in educational methods, condemn these same processes as stupid and old-fashioned, and advise the importation of European machinery as the only means of reviving this once flourishing Indian industry. But the fact that a scientific country like Germany interests itself in introducing these obsolete processes into her technical schools, ought to convince them that there are still possibilities in Indian handicraft which they have overlooked.

The moral I wish to draw is not that India is neglecting opportunities for developing export trade to Europe, but that she is allowing the most valuable industrial asset she possesses—the skill of her handicraftsmen—to degenerate, while European countries are spending great sums in endeavouring to regain that skill in handicraft which the abuse of mechanical appliances inevitably destroys.

What Europe is trying to regain by a costly system of industrial schools, India still possesses; for India is even now a great industrial country and possesses traditional schools of handicraft in every village workshop.

It is of vital importance for India to retain all this accumulated skill of hand and eye; *the problem for India is how to use labour-saving appliances not as a substitute for, but as an auxiliary to handicraft—so that handicraft may be developed instead of being crushed out by the inventions of modern science.* India will be the loser in every way if the further introduction of European inventions completes the destruction of her traditional handicraft; for India will then have to begin, as Europe has now begun, by a costly and tedious process, to recover that skill in handicraft which is just as essential to the progress of humanity as the development of mechanical science.

Before we can come to a rational conclusion as to what will be likely to improve the condition of Indian art and industry, we must thoroughly investigate the reasons which have led to their present state of stagnation and degeneration. The reasons are of various kinds, moral, intellectual and practical; but of these the moral and intellectual are very much the most important. India has lost self-respect and self-reliance; pride in her own artistic culture and faith in her spiritual mission. She hankers after the fleshpots of Egypt, and barters her birthright for a mess of pottage. Her young men, trained in Anglo-Indian schools and colleges, go to Europe with their artistic powers totally undeveloped, and, mostly in the squalid atmosphere of London boarding houses, obtain there a superficial knowledge of art, regarded only as a society amusement, not as the foundation of good living. They remain in total ignorance of those deeper undercurrents of artistic thought which make for true progress in Europe. They come back to India steeped in the decadent ideas of European materialism; with judgment warped and taste perverted, they are unable to understand either European art or Indian, and their only anxiety is to be considered fashionable and up-to-date. The fashions they follow are the fashions of decadent Europe—the common commercial art of the European shopkeeper. Art for them is even less real than it is for ordinary European society; it brings no beauty into their lives, and has no spiritual influence on their souls. Yet they have been the leaders of Indian artistic thought and in their hands lies the future of Indian art.

When, therefore, you ask me what can be done for Indian art I must tell you first you must learn to know what art is; and unless you know your own art —all that it has been for India, and all that it means —you will never know any art. Leave off asking Government to revive your art and industries: all that is worth having you must and can do for yourselves; and when you have achieved all that you can do, no Government would refuse to grant you the political rights you desire, for the development of your artistic faculties will give back to India the creative force her people have lost. It will infuse into all your undertakings the practical sense and power of organisation which are now so often wanting.

But you cannot know art truly by books or by any written word. All that I or any one else, can do for you is to advise you what are true artistic principles and what are false, and leave you to work out your own salvation; for men's creative powers of thought are only developed by thought and work, not by learning words by heart. Ruskin says: "The arts, as regards teachableness, differ from the sciences in this, that their power is founded not merely on facts which can be communicated, but on dispositions which require to be created." That disposition of thought which creates great art does not come by reasoning, but by intuition—by the power of the Spirit. All who love India must pray that the new spirit of which we hear so much may be that which inspires true art. If it be so, Indian art will become even greater and stronger than it ever was; for Indian art is not yet a withered tree. Its roots are still alive and healthy, and if those who care for it learn to do their duty to India, the sap may again be made to flow vigorously through its branches; the tree will revive and put forth its leaves and flowers with greater abundance than before.

Learn to know your own art before you seek to know what Europe thinks and does; let your own artists and craftsmen—those who have not forsaken the traditions of Indian art—be your artistic gurus, and when you have learnt all that they can teach you, you will find much that has been forgotten in your ancient literature and ancient monuments which will help both you and them to understand it better: for even your artists and craftsmen have much to learn of their own art. Their traditions are often corrupted, and you must go back to the purer sources of Samskṛṭ learning to really understand what they mean.

One of the characteristics of the true artistic spirit is that it makes those whom it inspires take delight in sharing with others the pleasure which art gives them. When you feel deeply that some thing is beautiful, you instinctively ask your neighbour to come and see it, and try to create in him the sense of the beauty you feel yourself, for the fellow-feeling in him adds to your own delight. The artistic spirit therefore is essentially a sociable one, and helps to develop the civic consciousness; and as I have said before, an art which is truly great strikes deep down into national life and has its roots in elemental ideas of order, decency and cleanliness. If therefore the new spirit is truly artistic, I should expect to find it manifesting itself not only in a desire to learn the meaning of Indian art, and what it has been in the past, but in the earnest endeavour to make others feel what art means and to share the gladness it brings with your fellow-creatures. A great art can only flourish when the people are glad, when they rejoice in their strength and can feel the beauty of life. And before India can feel glad again, the spirit of self-indulgence and distrust must give way to the spirit of mutual love and helpfulness; the people must set to work to put their houses in order, to help to cleanse their towns and villages and free the country from the curse of plague and malaria, to plant again the sacred trees as your religion bids you to do, and to purify and restore the tanks and wells which have been polluted or have fallen into decay. Art must become a part of your life and religion, as it has been before; and in this work European science can give you help—but that science must be made Indian, and a part of Indian religion, before it can fulfil its artistic purpose and make the people glad. Working towards this end science and art become one, for both will be inspired by an expression of that divine love which is the source of our being and the motive power of the Universe.

CHAPTER III

THE ADAPTATION OF INDIAN ART TO MODERN LIFE—INDIAN ARCHITECTURE

The stagnation of the creative faculties which is the root-cause of the decline of Indian art and industry is, as I have suggested, not only due to the limitation of foreign fashions and taste by the English-educated classes in India, though the same tendency in modern times has operated to the detriment of indigenous art and handicrafts in all Asiatic countries, and has affected all classes of people. The administrative system in India, more especially that of Public Works, has aggravated the evil greatly by ignoring indigenous art, but even this is only a contributory cause, not the paramount one. The fact that Public Works and other European fashions have had such a bad influence upon Indian art is only one of the symptoms of the disease, not the root-cause of it. And the rude shock which contact with western materialism has given to Indian thought and Indian institutions may, in the end, prove the salvation of Indian art by helping it to slough off all the evil influences which have been sapping its vitality for several centuries.

But the only way this can be brought about lies in giving back to Indian art its old place in Indian life and Indian religion: in adapting it to the new conditions and the new mode of life. Art must always be moving with the timds, for real art is the expression of the thought of the times. There is no finality in art in any age; it always needs the stimulus of new ideas to keep it healthy, just as the human body constantly requires fresh blood to be moving in the veins. An art which becomes merely imitative, instead of creative, necessarily decays because it lacks the stimulus of new thought. Indian art must be stimulated with new thought; but this cannot take place as long as educated India is content to be merely imitative.

Anglo-Indian education being merely imitative, cannot be of any use to Indian art. The fact that Indian art has been entirely ignored in the Anglo-Indian scheme of education has tended to hasten its decay only, because it has on that account led English-educated Indians to regard it with indifference or contempt. But even this neglect of art by the Universities may, in the end, prove an advantage by keeping Indian artists and craftsmen from being as much Anglicised and imitative as the Indians who have joined the literary, legal or scientific professions —provided that the awakening of the national consciousness which is now taking place makes India realise, before it is too late, all that she has to lose by the obliteration of her old artistic traditions.

It would be a fatal error to assume that Indian art traditions are now too old and worn out to be capable of adaptation to modern life and ways of thought. That would be a confession of intellectual and moral ineptitude which a self-respecting Indian should be ashamed to make. India has before experienced intellectual, political and social changes as great as those which have been brought about by the advent of western ideas and western Government. Indian art has never failed before to adapt itself to new conditions and even to acquire fresh vigour by the change of ideas; and India stands now in a better position than any European country for reconciling modern scientific ideas with ancient or modern art. The tendencies which have injured Indian art are those which must ultimately destroy all art, eastern or western; for they only go to substitute a sham art for a real one. If India, instead of merely imitating modern Europe, would set up for herself that higher ideal of science and art towards which the best thought of Europe is aiming, she would value her old artistic traditions far too highly to wish to throw them away.

Granted that in some ways Indian art has lost touch with modern life—the task which Indian reformers have to undertake is to teach their own artists and craftsmen to adapt their art to the new conditions. Take, for instance, the matter of dress—

it may be that the old Indian costumes are not always suitable for modern Indian modes of life, but is that a reason why educated Indians should substitute for it the most unbecoming and undignified costumes which Europeans have ever adopted? Are Indians really incapable of evolving a becoming and dignified dress, which shall be distinctively Indian, and at the same time suitable for modern ways of life? I am addressing myself more especially to the younger generation in this matter; for it is easy to understand that habits of life which have the sanction of several generations are not easily thrown aside, even for the sake of a higher ideal, by those who are advanced in years. No Indian young man who acts up to Swaḍeshi principles should ever appear in any other than a distinctively Indian dress, at least as long as he is on Indian soil. It is to the younger generation that we must look for the active stimulus which Indian art is in want of; though their elders may do much by their sympathy and encouragement.

In a thoughtful article on 'The Artistic Aspects of Dress,' published in the Ceylon *National Review* for January, 1907, Mr. Henry Holiday says:

In making a plea for greater beauty in our dress, I am pleading really for a greater spiritual beauty in our lives. As I have already said, we cannot separate Spirit from matter. A mind perpetually fed upon squalid forms, and gloomy, or gaudy colour, is a less beautiful mind than one that has been healthily nourished. Happily, we all have one antidote to the too-prevailing poison—we have Nature, we have blue sky, green trees and many coloured flowers. Our aim then must be to carry this beauty which surrounds us in Nature into our personal relations. Matter acts upon Spirit, and Spirit upon matter. A weary or diseased body will render the mind feeble and morbid; anxiety and failure tell upon our physical capacities. In like manner we cannot separate our inner life from its external manifestations. A low aim, a life spent in struggle for gain, will betray itself in an unlovely outside, and the cheerless, sunless surroundings with which we environ ourselves, will in their turn re-act upon our spirits and tend to remove us still further from healthy thought and emotions.

The West has done much that is noble. Its plastic arts, its music, its poetry and other literature stand at a very high level. Its science also has advanced in the last century as it never advanced before, but unfortunately its applied science, its mechanical progress, has been seized upon by money-makers and devoted to sordid ends, and before the baneful energy of this greedy horde the arts of daily life have gone down, giving place to gloom, monotony, clumsy formlessness and all that is hateful to lovers of beauty. We may in time alter this system which is fraught with such evil, and beauty may have a new birth in the West. *Meantime we look to the East for that which we have lost.*

Will the light of the East altogether fail us now, and will new India be content to run madly after the money bags of the West? If so, then assuredly India will not rise again in the scale of nations, except, after many more years of suffering and bitter experience, her people turn away in disgust from those who blindly and recklessly lead them astray.

It will be a hopeful sign for Indian art and Indian nationality when all young Indians take a pride in the beauty and dignity of their national dress. I believe that even in the few years since I left India there has been a considerable change for the better in this respect, which all Europeans who appreciate true culture must be glad to notice. Indians will certainly gain immensely, not only morally and intellectually, but even politically, by ceasing to imitate European fashions indiscriminately, for this very lack of discrimination which educated Indians have shown discredits them greatly in the eyes of Europe. Only when Indians can make Europe feel that they have as much to teach Europe as they have to learn from her, will they fully justify their claim for the same political rights as Europeans enjoy. As long as their chief ambition is to become successful imitators of what Europe does, they will remain in a state of political inferiority—and rightly so, for indiscriminate imitation is an admission of inferiority which inevitably depreciates the power of initiative and prevents the development of all the creative faculties.

To restore, then, the constructive powers of the Indian mind to their full capacity should be the first and chief aim of all Indian reformers and politicians. This aim, I must constantly repeat, can be attained much more effectively and quickly through the revival of national art and culture than by agitation for political rights. The experience and knowledge gained in constructive work of this kind will help much more than political agitation to develop those powers of mind which all men require for the due exercise of political rights when they are attained. Every Swaḍeshi politician should therefore begin by making his own home and his own village the exercising ground for his powers of constructive statesmanship, and thereby add not only to his own qualifications for Swaḍeshi citizenship, but increase both his own political influence and the political strength of the particular home and village to which he may belong.

Of all branches of art, that of architecture is the one which gives occasion for the exercise of the highest constructive powers, and in the revival of Indian domestic architecture there is a magnificent field open for the energy of the Swaḍeshi reformer, and the very best opportunity for giving a great stimulus to Indian art craft. Nowhere is it more true than in India that architecture is the mother of all the arts, and the neglect of Indian architectural traditions by Indian leaders of public opinion, has been one of the principal causes of the deterioration of Indian art.

It may be that English educated Indians find the old Indian style of house irksome and incompatible with their ideas of comfort. But why, instead of showing the Indian traditional builder how to adapt his design to new requirements, do they make him a bad imitator of inferior European architecture or employ Europeans to do that for them? If they act thus, with the idea that they are emulating the best achievements of Europe, they deceive themselves entirely, for no European house or palace yet built in this style would be considered as first-rate architecture in Europe, even compared with the best modern buildings. If they do so from a want of faith in Indian artistic capacity, it is a confession of impotence and failure, which is painful evidence of Indian intellectual degeneration, for never at any previous period of Indian history have Indian architects and craftsmen shown such incapacity.

It is only from ignorance of Indian architectural science that Anglo-Indians have assumed that it is not adaptable to the requirements of Anglo-Indian administration. Ignorance of things Indian is much less excusable in Indians than it is in Europeans. European experts like Fergusson, who have devoted themselves to the study of Indian architecture, acknowledge that the science of building has been developed by Indian architects to a point fully as high as, and in some instances higher than the best achievements of Europe. Fergusson further declared that if Indians could only be persuaded to take a pride in their own architecture, there could be no doubt that the master-builders of the present day who carry on the traditions of Indian architecture, might even now excel the great works of their ancestors, for he had learnt more of the real science of architecture, as practised by the great master-builders of Europe, by observing Indian master-builders at their work than he had learnt from all the works he had read. It is this want of pride and want of faith in their own traditional culture on the part of the upper classes of India, which has been much more destructive to Indian art than the ignorance or indifference of Europeans. That the decline of Indian art has not gone further than it has done is due chiefly to the spirituality of Indian women and the strong religious feeling of the 'uneducated' classes. Those who had always upheld the national artistic traditions as a part of their *ḍharma*, they constitute the true Swaḍeshi party.

If Indian art is to survive, it must always go hand in hand with religion. But I do not mean by this that Indians should do as Europeans often do when they attempt to adapt Indian art to practical uses, and borrow the forms of religious buildings for conversion to secular purposes. That is an offence against that sense of fitness which, as I explained in my first chapter, is one of the first principles of all applied art. The form of a house and of every part of it, must be prescribed by the use for which it is intended, as well as by the environment in which it is placed. If the forms prescribed by the old Indian architectural traditions are not suitable for modern uses, they must be altered, and you will find it will be much easier for an Indian builder to adapt his art to India than it is for a European builder to produce good art for you, for, as Fergusson said, the living Indian architectural traditions "are the result of the earnest thinking of thousands of minds spread over hundreds of years, and acting in unison with the national voice which called them into existence"—while architecture in Europe "is now little more than a dead corpse galvanised into life by a few selected practitioners for the amusement and delight of a small section of the specially educated classes. It is an art which is not conducted in truthful or constructive principle, but an imitative attempt to reproduce something which has no affinity with the building in hand." "Since the beginning of the sixteenth century," he said, "architects in Europe forsook the principles on which architecture and all other cognate arts had been practised from the beginning of time; they pursued common sense and common prudence, not in the hope of attaining greater convenience or greater effect, more easily or with less means, but in order to produce certain associations with which education had made them familiar." That is exactly what English-educated Indians have been doing when they have tried to build their houses and palaces on European models. But they have far less excuse for producing bad architecture than we have in Europe, where the sound architectural traditions of the Middle Ages and splendid craftsmanship have become almost extinct while in India you have still alive the living traditions of the finest architectural schools, and schools of craftsmanship the world has ever known.

A great deal could be said upon the subject of architecture, for national architecture is built out of the national life; its forms and style are moulded by the character of the people to whom it belongs, and the character of every individual is affected by the environment he makes for himself, or allows to be made for him, in his own house. It is not merely a question of taste that is involved in the preservation of Indian art, but a question of intellectual and moral character. The surrender of all their artistic traditions, which so many educated Indians have been content to make, is an intellectual and moral loss for which all European science and literature cannot compensate them; nor will the fullest measure of political liberty, as it is understood by western nations, restore to them what they lose by that surrender. India with Indian art completely denationalised by western commercialism and western materialism will still remain in a state of intellectual and moral servitude, even if all the dreams of swarāj in which the extremists indulge were realised; but India with all the vitality of its national art renewed would be politically much more powerful than now, even though the present bureaucratic form of government remained unchanged.

For stimulating the revival of Indian art I have no heroic measures to propose, no great scheme to lay before you for debate in public meeting. If India is really, as it seems to be, on the eve of a great national awakening, the stimulus required is there already, and all that India now requires is clear-sightedness to discriminate between what is valuable and what is worthless in the teaching of the West, and to attain to a full understanding of the value of her old artistic traditions, joined with a willingness on the part of each individual to do what may be within his or her scope, to restore all forms of Indian art to their former place in the national life, and to help to mould them to the new ideas which are creating new wants and new aspirations.

But English-educated Indians, especially, will have difficulties to encounter, owing more to their own past indifference to Indian art than to the incapacity of Indian artists and craftsmen. It will not be easy for you to persuade Indian builders and craftsmen, when you ask them to adapt their work to your requirements and taste, that you do not now mean them to imitate European models, but to produce something better, or something which shall be modern and useful, but still Indian. You have taught them so long to believe that this imitation of European models is in your eyes the highest art, that it will take some time to eradicate the bad influence of these imitative ideas. Neither will it be easy for you yourselves with your best will, to acquire the sense of fitness and the sense of beauty which will enable you to exercise wisely your judgments in artistic matters. Nor should you depend entirely upon your own individual judgment, but rather let national artistic tradition be your guide, for national tradition represents the ripened judgment and experience of many generations, and is not to be thrown aside at the mere caprice of individual taste, from the desire of novelty, or at the dictates of fashions foreign to your country and ways of life. Study carefully your old traditions and try to understand the reason for them, for they are nearly always founded on reason and common sense. Perhaps in some cases the conditions which give rise to them may have altered, and the reasons which formerly existed are no longer applicable. But even in such cases it is better to rely upon the trained experience of the craftsman to make the necessary alterations, rather than to impose your own judgment upon him.

I would strongly advise you in this connection, to study carefully a little book on the Indian craftsman, by Dr. Coomaraswamy, with an introduction by Mr. C. R. Ashbee, a well-known architect who has been the moving spirit in the work of the Guild of Handicraft at Campden. Mr. Ashbee says:

It is a curious and suggestive thought that the spiritual reawakening in England, which goes now by the name of the higher culture, now by the name of Socialism, which has been voiced in our time by Ruskin and Morris, which has expressed itself in movements like the Arts and Crafts, or is revealed in the inspired paintings of the Pre-Raphaelites, demands just such a condition as in India our commercialisation is destroying. The spiritual reawakening in the West is appealing for a social condition in which each man shall have not only an economic but a spiritual status in the society in which he lives, or as some of us would prefer to put it, he shall have a stable economic status in order that he may have a spiritual status as well. It is such a condition which still exists in India, where Society is organised, as Dr. Coomaraswamy shows, upon a basis of "personal responsibility and co-operation" instead of, as with us, upon a basis of contract and competition. Even if we admit that the change of the Āryan in the West from one basis to the other has been necessary to produce the conditions of modern progress, the scientific results of our civilisation .... it may yet be that the spiritual reawakening that is beginning to stir the dry bones of western materialism may yet leave the East fundamentally unchanged, and bring us again into some kindred condition through our contact with her.

Here you can observe again the anxiety of social reformers in Europe to preserve and revive the very economic conditions which have survived much more largely in the East than in the West; those which many so-called Swaḍeshi reformers in India are now using their influence to replace by a further extension of European commercialism. Says Mr. Ashbee:

"There has come over our western civilisation," "in the last twenty-five years, a green-sickness, a nausea, an unrest; it is not despondency, for in the finer minds it takes the form of an intense spiritual hopefulness; but it takes the form also of a profound disbelief in the value of the material conditions of modern progress, a longing to sort the wheat from the chaff, the serviceable from the useless, a desire to return from mechanical industry and its wastefulness, and to look once more to the human hand, to be once again with Mother Earth."

It makes me almost despair of Indian spirituality to find so many of the leaders of new India actively propagating the extension of the modern factory system in India, instead of devoting all their energies to reorganising and developing the industrial side of Indian communal life in an Indian way. Dr. Coomaraswamy says:

"Certain short-sighted Swaḍeshists desire an increase of production in Indian industries, at whatever cost of reckless exploitation of the worker's forces. But the exploitation of the physique and life of the Indian people for a temporary trade advantage is a mistaken policy; and Indians must demand and obtain a regulation of the conditions of labour on this account, quite apart from the fact that English manufacturers may be acting from motives of quite a different character."

It is on this point especially that new India requires clearer thinking and a deeper insight into those movements in Europe which are making for true progress. If all the misplaced energy which has been devoted, especially in Bengal, to the establishment of 'Swaḍeshi' cotton mills had been directed towards the revival of village industry and Indian domestic architecture, the Swaḍeshi movement would have benefited India much more than it has done. For, as Mr. Ashbee truly says, the Indian craftsmen and the Indian village community have a definite and necessary place, not only in the Indian order of things, not only in the culture of the East, but in the world.

Here once more we are learning from the East. The English craftsmen and the English village are passing, or have passed away; and it is only in quite recent times that we have discovered that they, too, are counterparts one of the other. Industrial machinery, blindly misdirected, has destroyed them both, and recent English land-legislation has been trying, with allotment and small-holdings acts, to re-establish the broken village life. Those of us, however, who have studied the arts and crafts, in their town and country conditions, are convinced that the small-holding problem is possible of solution only by some system of co-operation, and if some forms of craftsmanship are simultaneously revived and added to it. "Speak to the earth and it shall teach thee;" that is an old lesson, and it is true not only of England, but of all western countries that have been touched by the green-sickness of industrial machinery. With us in the West it is the newest of new ideas that the arts and crafts and the revival of agriculture are the corollary of one another. In India they always appear to have thought this, and to have held by the truth.

Let new India learn all that the old India has to teach before it attempts to profit by the wisdom of the West.

CHAPTER IV

FINE ART AND ITS REVIVAL IN INDIA

THE distinction which is now made between 'Fine Art' and 'Industrial or Applied Art,' is a quite modern one, and one of which the East has hardly ever been conscious. It is an untrue and unnecessary distinction, indicative of much that is unhealthy and artificial in modern life, and in the greatest epochs of European art the distinction was never made. The same influences which have caused Indian architecture to decline have affected Indian sculpture and painting to an even greater extent—the spread of western materialism and the neglect by educated Indians of their own traditional culture. In my *Indian Sculpture and Painting* I have endeavoured to show that the position of inferiority which Europe has always attributed to Indian artists, in respect to the higher aspects of art, has been entirely due to a misconception of their aims, and to a misunderstanding of the eastern outlook upon nature. This misconception would not have existed so long, had it not been that the great majority of educated Indians have always tacitly accepted the position of inferiority which European opinion has accorded to Indian fine art, and made no attempt to enlighten Europe as to the true Indian point of view.

I received a short time ago a long and interesting letter from a Bengali correspondent which shows me that some of the passages in my book have been misunderstood. I will therefore endeavour to make my position clearer on the points to which he takes exception. My correspondent writes: "My first feeling on reading your book was to protest against a few sentences therein (p. 53): 'The female type is also taken by Indian artists to personify divine fury and destructive energy, in the form of Durga, the fighting Goddess, who wars against demons and spirits of evil, and Kāli, mother of all the Gods, and destroyer of the Universe. The latter, in modern Hindū art, is a hideous, vulgar conception, altogether unworthy of the noble artistic traditions of earlier times.'" "This may mean," my correspondent continues, "that in modern Hindū art Kāli is hideously represented, or it may mean that Kāli is a modern conception and it is hideous and vulgar. . . . where lies the hideousness, and the vulgarity you speak of? Does it lie in the nakedness, or in the dangling tongue? You seem to have taken it for granted that the female type is taken to represent the 'Divine fury and destructive energy' alone. This assertion conclusively proves that this piece of our art has not been studied by you in the same spirit as you may have done the others. . . Mother Kāli is the soul of a divine worship which has produced more than half the very best hymns and songs in the living Bengali language, a divine worship which has produced an endless host of Buḍḍha-like men in Bengal, lastly a Srī Rāmakṛṣhṇa of Dakhineshwar (whose life has been written by the late Professor Max Müller), and Swami Vivekānanḍa, whose thoughts on Hinḍū religion and the practical Veḍānṭa philosophy are palpably conquering the cream of the intellectual world. In the name of Sacred Art, I charge you to make atonement for the Veḍānṭic criticism on it by expunging it from the book. This sentence has raised a great murmur."

I fear my correspondent, in the fervour of his religious zeal, is allowing his judgment to go astray. He admits that my words may bear two different constructions but, without waiting for further explanation, he fastens upon them the least obvious of the two, and calls upon me to withdraw a proposition which I have not, and never had, the least wish to maintain. The intention of my book is purely artistic, and when I wrote that "Kāli, *in modern Hinḍū art*, is a hideous, vulgar conception" it did not occur to me that any one would interpret those words as an attack upon the abstract idea, or religious conception of Kāli. What I meant was that modern Hinḍū art represented Kāli in a manner quite unworthy (artistically) of the high abstract ideas which intellectual Hinḍūs associate with the name. A work of art should convey, even to an outsider, an adequate impression of the ideas it represents; but in the case of modern images of Kāli I do not think that anyone, except one of her own devotees, would associate high religious ideals with the artistic representations which are now made of her. I do not object to the nakedness of these images, nor to the protruding tongue: neither of these attributes is incompatible with great art. But I do maintain that the makers of these images fail completely to translate into concrete form what my correspondent describes as "the grand combination of feelings embodied in the conception of Kāli".

I would go further and maintain that the same failure is conspicuous, in perhaps a lesser degree, in all modern Hinḍū images. They all, without exception, fall far behind the great master-pieces of Hinḍū art, illustrated in my book, which European artists can thoroughly appreciate as worthy representations of high religious ideals; and I would ask my Hinḍū readers to earnestly consider this matter, for a deterioration of art is always an indication of spiritual and intellectual degeneration—and this deterioration set in long before the advent of British rule, to which some of your thinkers are too ready to attribute all the evils for which India suffers at the present day. It can be observed, not only in Hinḍū sculpture but in the lesser arts—in the vessels and symbols you use in your worship, and in domestic appliances as well. There is less sincerity in the workmanship, a diminished sense of beauty in the forms and decoration, less simplicity and dignity in the style, than there were in such things even fifty years ago: but the deterioration did not begin then, it dates from times anterior to the introduction of western ideas and western government, though undoubtedly it has been much more rapid in recent times.

I ventured in my book to suggest some of the influences, other than western materialism and commercialism, which have helped to bring about this degeneration in Hinḍū art. One was, undoubtedly, the puritanical ideas of the Muhammaḍan religion, which laid a ban upón the higher forms of art, as being irreligious—just as many Christian puritans have done. This limitation of artistic expression must inevitably lead to deterioration, intellectual and spiritual, for the artistic faculty is the highest of spiritual gifts and the reverent exercise of it in the worship of God will always be the source of its highest inspiration. But these puritanical ideas have not been confined to Muhammaḍan and Christian teachers, and I believe we must look for the deeper reason of the decline of Hinḍū art in the decline of religious feeling in Hinḍūism, just as the true explanation of the decline of Christian art is to be found in a decline of the Christian faith.

I tried to suggest in my book that there are some aspects of Hindū philosophy which might have an inherent tendency to bring about a stagnation in the creative faculties. I wrote (p. 81) :

> Obviously the Vedāntic doctrine of Māyā, which treats all nature as illusion, might, if pushed to extremes, cut away the ground of all artistic creation, just as the intense mental concentration, which is the foundation of the Yoga school of philosophy, might eventually lead to absolute quietism and intellectual sterility.

My correspondent takes this to mean that the doctrine of Māyā and the practice of yoga *necessarily* lead to intellectual sterility, and rather indignantly asks : "Did Buddha have intellectual sterility; did Shaṇkarāchāryā ; or did Vivekānanda, or Srī Rāmakrṣhṇa Paramahamsa?

This was very far from my meaning. What I wished to express was that though the practice of yoga does not, as I am fully aware, necessarily mean asceticism, it does tend to withdraw a great many active minds from worldly affairs, and that the continual concentration of the human mind upon the Real and Absolute, does, in many cases, lead men to despise the unreality and impermanence of this present existence, to neglect their duties as citizens and to cease to exercise their intellectual faculties in the affairs of this life. Certainly the great spiritual teachers, whose names my correspondent cites, did not fall into such a state ; but that was because their practice of yoga was inspired by the deepest love for their fellow-men, and through this love it became intellectually fruitful in the highest degree. Without such love, which, as I said in my first chapter, is always the motive power of the highest art creation, the yoga practice of ordinary men often leads to intellectual sterility; for faculties which are withdrawn from constant exercise tend to become atrophied, just as any muscle of the body will become atrophied when it is never exerted.

So far from arguing that the practice of yoga is necessarily destructive to art creation, I have tried in my book to show that the power of spiritual insight, which the practiser of yoga endeavours to develop, is the fundamental principle in Indian art. I would go even further and maintain that this power of spiritual insight is the foundation of all the highest art, whether it be eastern or western; and so it is that the greatest European artists and thinkers have received their inspiration from yoga, often without being conscious of it and without practising the specialised spiritual exercises which are part of the Indian yogi's ritual. My correspondent gives me an interesting anecdote which, he says, "will illustrate the way of art conception of the Hindūs and prove that the practice of yoga alone gives the best artistic conceptions and does not bring about intellectual sterility, as you say". I would adopt the same anecdote to show that there is no fundamental difference between the highest art conceptions in the East and the West. The eastern artists practise yoga consciously, the western generally unconsciously; but the European who possesses artistic insight can thoroughly appreciate Indian art, even though he may be entirely ignorant of Indian philosophy and religious practices.

A man who did not know Samskṛṭ but practised religion, and hence a practiser of yoga, used often to read the *Gīṭā* without understanding a bit of it, and would shed tears as he read it. A Brāhmaṇa who was a paṇḍiṭ, often passed by and observed this man reading the *Gīṭā* with tears in his eyes. He found out that the man did not understand Samskṛṭ, and so he was curious to know why the man wept while he read a thing he did not understand at all. So the Brāhmaṇa one day put the question to him and the man replied. "Oh Sir! when I read the sacred book I see Bhagavān Srī Kṛshṇa as Pārṭhasāraṭhi telling the *Gīṭā* to Arjuna, and I cannot help weeping at the glorious sight!" The proud paṇḍiṭ fell at his feet and said: *Vayam taṭṭwānveshāt naṭāh, maḍhukara ṭwam khaṭu kriti*—"While we are dead by our search after the truth, Sir, thou art blessed as the bee, successful in finding it!"

I fully agree, however, with my correspondent when he says that "photography and the tenth-rate commerical art of Europe" are propagating quite a wrong grammar of art in India. 'Fine art Societies' and English education do the same; but it is not right to attribute the decay of Indian art entirely to western influence. If there had not been esoteric influences tending to degeneration in Indian art, it would have remained sufficiently sure of its position to resist destructive exoteric influences—it could have exposed the wrongness of the foreign grammar itself and not have taken it on trust as better than its own. As I have said before, it is possible, even probable, that the shock of the contact with western materialism was just the force needed to revive what is worth reviving in Indian art and to help it to slough off what is worthless—the force which should rouse India to reconsider her position and to make that readjustment which, as the *Gīṭā* says, must be made " whenever there is low vibration in the spirit of religion ".

" Swāmi Vivekānanḍa used to say," (writes my correspondent) " with regard to the relations of England to India: 'the snake which has bitten must again suck out the poison if the patient is destined to survive.' Here, in the case of art, England, consciously or unconsciously killed Indian art, and when you, an Englishman, have sucked out the heinous poison, I take it to be significant of future art revival."

If I am to play the part of physician to Indian art I would take a less desponding view of the patient's state than my correspondent does. Indian art is still very much alive, at least as much as art is in Europe, and while I am doing my best to suck out the western poison, I think it my duty to tell the patient that the poison would never have acted so violently were it not for the unhealthiness of the body before the snake came to bite it. The snake venom, however, may after all prove to be the true antitoxin to the poison of the previous sickness, and India may yet learn to bless the great Nāga of the West under whose shelter its national consciousness is now re-awakening. It is only the excess of the poison which has done so much harm, and when India returns to its normal state I believe that its art will achieve even greater things than it has done before. The greatest danger both to India and to England, is from the spread of race-antagonism, a poison even more fatal to human progress than the poison of materialism.

I am again in agreement with my correspondent when he says: "Music is the most potent factor in the harmonious development of art." I shall have occasion to refer to this point later on when I come to the question of education. Music is the soul of art, but neither music, nor any other intellectual or spiritual force, should be used to promote the feeling of race-antagonism. It is false music, and false art which create hatred and discord instead of love and harmony.

Though I always insist strongly upon the importance of the industrial side of art—upon the necessity of making art a part of life and work—you must not think that the higher branches of painting and sculpture are not to be considered of great account in the political economy of art. On the contrary, the condition of the fine arts gives the surest indication of the soundness or unsoundness of the whole artistic life of a people, and the generally miserable state of the fine arts in India is the worst symptom of the decadence, just as the beginning of a new School of Indian painting, of which there are encouraging indications in Bengal, is the most hopeful sign of a general renaissance of art. So while Swaḍeshi reformers are interesting themselves in industrial schemes, they should not believe that the state of the fine arts is not worth their attention. Utility and beauty must go hand in hand: neither should be exalted at the expense of the other. Ruskin has wisely written, in his *Political Economy of Art*, that in the plans of the perfect economist, or mistress of the household,

> there is a studied expression of the balanced division of her care between the two great objects of utility and splendour; in her right hand, food and flax, for life and clothing; in her left hand, the purple and the needlework, for honour and for beauty. All perfect housewifery or national economy is known by these two divisions; wherever either is wanting the economy is imperfect. If the motive of pomp prevails, and the care of the national economist is directed only to the accumulation of gold, and of pictures, and of silk and marble, you know at once that the time must soon come when all these treasures shall be scattered and blasted in national ruin. If, on the other hand, the element of utility prevails, and the nation disdains to occupy itself in anywise with the arts of beauty and delight, not only a certain quantity of its energy calculated for exercise in those arts alone must be entirely wasted, which is bad economy, but also the passions connected with the utilities of property

become morbidly strong, and a mean lust of accumulation merely for the sake of accumulation, or even of labour merely for the sake of labour, will banish at last the serenity and morality of life, as completely, and perhaps more ignobly, than even the lavishness of pride, and the lightness of pleasure. And similarly, and much more visibly, in private and household economy, you may judge always of its perfectness by its fair balance between the use and the pleasure of its possessions. You will see the wise cottager's garden trimly divided between its well-set vegetables and its fragrant flowers; you will see the good housewife taking pride in her pretty table-cloth, and her glittering shelves, no less than in her well dressed dish, and her full store-room; the care in her countenance will alternate with gaiety, and though you will reverence her in her seriousness, you will know her best by her smile.

But before the higher branches of art can be restored to a sound and vigorous state, they too must be made a part of life and work, contributing to the national well-being and happiness, just as much as the industrial arts. The fine arts in India have degenerated into an amusement for the rich, a means of gratifying personal vanity and pride; they must become a part of national education and be made to serve the highest aims of religion and life. The collecting of European pictures, which is one of the amusements of the aristocracy and plutocracy in India, does not promote art or the morality of life: it is merely a competition in ostentation and self-indulgence. To quote Ruskin's words again: "It is hardly possible to spend your money in a worse or more wasteful way; for though you may not be doing it for ostentation yourself, you are, by your pertinacity, nourishing the ostentation of others; you meet them in their game of wealth, and continue it for them; if they had not found an opposite player the game would have been done; for a proud man can find no enjoyment in possessing himself of what nobody disputes with him."

Even when regarded merely as an investment, it is always a bad one—"an investment in a cargo of mental quicklime or guano, which being laid on the fields of human nature, is to grow a harvest of pride."

The old Indian picture and sculpture galleries, such as those at Ajanta, Amaravaṭi and Ellora, as well as the *chiṭrasālas,* the private galleries of the aristocracy, were schools of religion, of morality, of national culture and history. There will never be a true renaissance of art in India until the fine arts are restored to their proper place in the national life. Your children should learn the stories of Rāmā and Sīṭā, of Kṛshṇa and Rāḍhā, of Sāviṭri and Saṭyavan, of Nala and Ḍamayanṭi, not only from books, but from pictures painted on the walls of your schools, houses and palaces. Your young men should take lessons in religion and history from great paintings on the walls of colleges and municipal buildings. And these must be painted by Indian artists and in an Indian way. This is the part which fine art should take in a complete and sound scheme of national education.

There are many Indian artists to be found who have not forgotten the Indian way of painting and sculpture, and if those who wish to encourage Indian art would lead them to work in this way, instead of wasting money in prizes, at Fine Art Exhibitions, or in sending young men to Europe to learn European ideas of art, there would soon be no need of any other schools of art in India. I have often heard it said that the caste system has been one of the reasons of the degeneration of Indian Fine Art. Whatever may be said against the caste system, this cannot justly be maintained. But for the caste system the traditional artistic culture, which gives the present generation of Indians such splendid foundation to build upon, would long ago have disappeared entirely. It is almost impossible to overvalue the importance of a sound tradition in art. As Dr. Coomaraswamy rightly says (*Mediæval Sinhalese Art,* p. 98):

It does not prevent the man of genius from producing the most beautiful work possible, though ensuring that it shall so far conform to an accepted standard as to be immediate and universal in its appeal; at the same time it does prevent the possibility of holy and elevating subjects being treated absurdly or stupidly, so as to wound the feelings of serious men; which happens every day now that the old tradition is generally broken with. . . . . Even the worst traditional work is preferable to the weak, effeminate and sensuous drawing of low-country workmen [in Ceylon], who under western influence have attempted a more naturalistic style without any training, and certainly without taste.

And again (p. 171) he says:

It must not be supposed, however, that tradition, by its very nature, fetters the expression and production of great art; on the contrary it enables the great artists to speak in a language understanded of the people, and without that necessity for explanation which reduces the value of more individualistic art; and the existence of an art language is no more a fetter to the true artist than the existence of a word language is to the true poet. And what did tradition mean to the lesser craftsmen, for whom art was but a craft? It gave them a conception so defined as to avoid all danger of the sacred subjects being treated absurdly or irreverently. How well this aim was attained is shown by the vulgarity and stupidity that do appear in Indian art, where the tradition is rudely and contemptuously broken. But while the tradition lasted, it saved the man of small capacity from his own folly, and made it possible for him to work acceptably within its limits.

Because this sound artistic tradition exists it does not follow that the practice of painting and sculpture and of other arts, should continue to be confined to the hereditary artistic castes. In the greatest periods of Indian art this was never the case. There are innumerable passages in Samskṛt and Pāli literature which show that painting was often practised by kings and princes as well as by professional artists. It will be a very healthy sign when the aristocracy of India, instead of collecting European pictures for the purpose of display, begin to practise the arts themselves, as they did in former days. First let the traditional artists be restored to the honoured position they formerly held in Indian Courts, and to a dignified position in society as the upholders of national artistic tradition, and you will not then want European teachers to instruct you in art.

The princes and aristocracy of India have a great responsibility in this matter, for on their patronage the prosperity of the fine arts largely depends. All educated Indians should feel that by dishonouring the Indian artists who hold to their ancient traditions they are dishonouring art, dishonouring India, and dishonouring themselves. The honour you mete out to Indian artists should not be in proportion to their skill in imitating European art—the essence of art is creation, not imitation—but in proportion to their ability to interpret truly Indian life and Indian artistic thought. By putting Indian fine art on a lower intellectual plane than that of Europe you lower the whole intellectual vitality of India, for nothing is more intellectually depressing than the feeling of a constitutional inferiority.

Indians will never recover their intellectual freedom until art takes again its former place in national education, and until that intense feeling for beauty, and that love and reverence for nature, which shine so strongly in Veḍic literature, inspire once more the whole national life and religion, just as it once inspired the life and thought of Greece and Italy—and of all countries where art has ever flourished. Every great intellectual awakening, since the world began, has proceeded from this *yoga*—communion with the source of all beauty, and all love, which your old Ṛṣhis taught and practised, whose wisdom is your most precious heritage. So, while you give your artistic traditions their rightful honour and place in your national education you must not consider them all-sufficient for you, but go yourselves direct to the same source, from which their inspiration was drawn, *for there only will you and your children imbibe the strength and refreshment which will revive your art.*

You must inculcate in your children the love of beauty in nature and in art by making the environment of your schools and colleges beautiful with trees and flowers and pleasant pools of water, as they were in the great days of Indian art. Read the description which Hiouen T'sang, the Chinese pilgrim, gave of the famous convent of Nalanḍa, one of the old Indian Universities:

> All around, pools of translucent water shone with the open petals of the blue lotus flowers; here and there the lovely kanaka trees hung down their deep red blossoms; and woods of dark mango trees spread their shade between them. In the different courts, the houses of the monks were each four stories in height. The pavilions had pillars ornamented with dragons, and beams resplendent with all the colours of the rainbow—rafters richly carved, columns ornamented with jade, painted red and richly chiselled, and balustrades of carved open-work.

You might take a lesson, too, from the national life of the Japanese, who always celebrate the blooming of the iris flowers and of the cherry blossom as a great national festival for young and old. Should not India have her lotus flower day, and asoka blossom day—days to be associated with the planting of flowering trees and fruit trees for the public good and pleasure, and with the dedication of beautiful wall-paintings in schools and colleges and municipal buildings? For assuredly the power of knowing beauty and loving it is a moral and intellectual faculty of as much importance in national education as reading, writing and arithmetic; and if there is one fact which history clearly teaches, it is, that national life is always strongest and most healthy when the national artistic instincts are most developed.

The Greeks knew this, and based their whole educational system upon it; our present English system of classical education, while professing to take Greek culture for its model, persistently ignores the whole spirit of it by treating the æsthetic faculties as of very small importance. The Greek system of education had no room for the minute dissection of dead languages; its scheme of mental gymnastics hardly took cognisance of book-learning at all—at least not in the form in which it is used in Anglo-Indian schools—but it regarded as of vital importance the development of the sense of rhythm, or the bringing of the mental, moral and physical faculties of the individual into perfect tune with the eternal harmony of nature In fact, it devoted its whole attention to the very faculties which are almost completely neglected in the usual modern European system of education.

Modern European educationists are only now beginning to realise that education to the Greek did not mean the stuffing of the youthful brain with a more or less complete knowledge of scientific 'facts,' nor the unscientific exercise of the body in more or less disorderly sports (which are by no means the best adapted for producing a *mens sana in corpore sano*), but the development of a sense of perfect harmony in all the relations of human life—intellectual, moral and physical; and as the essence of nature's harmony is contained in poetry, music and art, these subjects took the principal place in a young man's mental and moral education, while physical education was also based upon the practice of rhythmic exercises having for their object the most perfect development of the whole organisation of the human body, rather than the cultivation of the sporting instinct. For the purpose of a sound physical education the old Indian system of exercises is much better adapted than English cricket and foot-ball, though for developing strength of character a good deal may be said for the English games.

Educational reformers in India should endeavour to work in the true scientific spirit of Greek education, instead of imitating modern European pedagogic systems, which are only classical in name. They should follow Plato's advice.

Seek out such workmen as are able by the help of a good natural genius to trace the nature of the beautiful and the decent, that our youth, dwelling as it were in a healthful place, may be profited at all hands: whence from the beautiful works, something will be conveyed to the sight and hearing, as a breeze bringing health from salutary places, imperceptibly leading them on directly from childhood to the resemblance, friendship, and harmony with right reason.

All the arts, said Plato, should be used for this rhythmical training of the human faculties.

Painting, too, is full of these things, and every other workmanship of the kind; and weaving is full of these, and carving, and architecture and all workmanship of every kind of vessels—as is, moreover, the nature of bodies and of all vegetables: for in all these there is propriety and impropriety; and the impropriety, discord and dissonance are the sisters of ill expression and ill sentiment, and their opposites are the sisters and imitations of sober and good sentiment.

It will be convenient, before commencing to deal more fully with educational questions, to give a summary of my practical proposals for the revival of Indian Architecture and the fine arts of painting and sculpture.

I. Let every Indian, who builds a house or palace, do honour to Indian art by employing Indian master-builders who have the knowledge of Indian architectural traditions contained in the Shilpa-Shāstras. Let him in consultation with these master-builders, adapt these traditions to present-day habits and requirements as they have always been adapted in former times; bearing in mind that the fundamental principle of good art is that perfect fitness makes perfect beauty. Let good ornament be used, as far as means will allow, only to add to the beauty of suitable design and good construction; never for the purpose of concealing ugliness, or defects, nor for the sake of vulgar display. Good design and construction make all work artistic, even if no ornament be added.

II. Let all furniture and decoration made for Indian houses, even chairs and similar furniture of European origin, be made distinctively Indian in design, not merely imitative of European forms; and let Indian dress be worn by Indians in Indian houses. So will you and your craftsmen develop your creative and constructive powers of thought.

III. To promote national reverence for beauty in nature and in art, let it be considered a public duty to make the surroundings of schools and public buildings beautiful with flowers and trees and water.

IV. Let days be set apart, as in Japan, for the national enjoyment and worship of beauty—days to celebrate the flowering of the lotus, or asoka tree, and for visiting places conspicuous for natural beauty.

V. Let religious festivals and political meetings be marked as much by the planting of fruit and flowering trees for the public benefit as by prayers and vows and speech-making. If for every speech now made a tree were planted and made to grow, how much happier would India become! Will not the Industrial Section of the National Congress inaugurate an Arbor-Day for all India, on the basis of one, two or three trees planted and made to grow, for every political speech delivered—the ratio to be determined by the length of the speeches?

VI. Let the great events of national history, and the moral teaching of the national epics, be impressed strongly on the minds of your children by concrete images painted on the walls of school and municipal buildings, instead of only by word-impressions derived from books and oral teaching. But such pictures must always be painted by Indian artists, with Indian colours and in the Indian way of artistic expression.

VII. Let the rich men of India show an intelligent interest in art, not by collecting European pictures, but by taking care of the masterpieces of Indian art, and by reviving the old *chiṭrashālās*, in which Indian subjects are painted on the walls by Indian artists in an Indian way.

The best way to honour Indian architects, sculptors, and painters is by giving them honourable employment; so it is very necessary to find out and bring to public notice all the traditional master-builders and sculptors who are now practising the rules of their art in the traditional Indian way, and all descendants of the painters who formerly held honoured positions at Indian Courts. I know that a good many very able architects and sculptors are still working in Northern India; even in Calcutta, where Indian artistic traditions have been almost obliterated by the influence of modern education and commercialism, I discovered an able young artist, compelled for want of other remunerative employment to make patterns for Manchester piece-goods, whose grandfather had been Court painter to the Nawāb of Murshidabad! I secured him an appointment in the Calcutta School of Art, as a teacher of painting. He has done very good teaching work there, and his own art has improved very much in the more artistic environment in which he is now placed. There are certainly a good many of such artists wanting work, still to be found living in obscurity, owing to the degeneration of public taste in India.

These are just the men whose knowledge of traditional Indian art is of the greatest value, but they are becoming fewer every year, and with them the most precious traditions of Indian architecture, sculpture and painting will become extinct. It is the obvious duty of every Indian who professes interest in art, to exert himself to bring such men and their work into public notice. The Industrial section of the Indian Congress, which has done valuable work with regard to Indian industries, should take a broader view of the artistic interests of India, and not restrict its efforts to what are commonly called the 'useful' arts. All art is useful.

The Indian Society of Oriental Art at Calcutta—which is the only Fine Art Society in India whose annual Exhibitions are organised on thoroughly sound lines—has hitherto found considerable difficulty in its endeavours to bring Indian artists into public notice. The scope of its work would be very much extended if it received more active support from Indians. The Madras Presidency, and every other province in India ought to have similar societies. Whatever may be said of the sun-dried bureaucrat and his indifference to art, it must be acknowledged by every fair-minded Indian, even those whose political views are most extreme, that up to the present time Indian art has received quite as much moral and material support from Anglo-Indians, in their non-official capacity, as it has received from the majority of educated Indians. It is the privilege of the artist to occupy neutral ground in politics, and I sincerely believe, in spite of Mr. Kipling, that in working together for the revival of Indian art, Europeans and Indians may find that sphere of common interest in which political, racial and social animosities and prejudices may be completely forgotten.

In no part of the world does the vitality of art depend entirely on the action or inaction of Government; official art is nearly always bad art. True art is the full expression of the individual or national consciousness, and is primarily the concern of each individual and of the community at large, rather than of the administrative machinery. Departmentalism is indifferent to art only when the people are so.

CHAPTER V

EDUCATION AND NATIONAL CULTURE

Education, in the common acceptance of the word, is taken to be synonymous with school teaching, though every educationist will admit that a great part, even the most vital part of education, is connected with an environment of influences in early life over which the schoolmaster or mistress often has no control. In all sound systems of education, national culture—the traditions of national life and thought—must harmonise entirely with the school and University teaching which should only be complementary or supplementary of the other. The fault of the Anglo-Indian educational system—the heinous and completely damning fault which has not been removed by recent attempts at reform—is that instead of harmonising with, and supplementing, national culture, it is completely antagonistic to and destructive of it.

The system, which, as Sir George Birdwood lately said, "has destroyed in Indians the love of their own literature, the quickening soul of a people, and their delight in their own arts, and worst of all, their repose in their own traditional and national religion, has disgusted them with their own homes, their parents, their sisters, their very wives, and brought discontent into every family so far as its baneful influences have reached". This system, whether you call it National, or whether you call it Anglo-Indian, is hopelessly and irrevocably condemned both in Europe and in India. It is at the same time perilous to the British Rāj by its antagonism to national traditions, and absolutely fatal to the national aspirations of Indians; for even were an Indian Governor-General installed at Simla and Indian Parliaments opened at Madras, Calcutta, Bombay and Lahore, Indians, by the loss of all their national culture, would still be as much subject to Europe as they are now, for the intellectual pivot of the world would be, even more than it is now, fixed in the western hemisphere.

Intellect is, and always will be, the ruling force in the world. You will never achieve political independence by Europeanising your intellects; you will only fasten still more firmly the bonds of your political subjection. A correspondent of the *Hindū,* referring to this argument, says that I confuse cause and consequence. He writes:

Indian ideals are nearly destroyed because we are nowhere politically, and we can't control the shaping of the ideals of our young men and women in the schools and colleges—social, or artistic, or religious. These are essentially national ideals, and the only method by which they can be made great or living must be political. The national consciousness comes to itself through politics. Political reform must be the vision of nationalist; politics first—and then our artistic life shall gain its place in the world's life and become aware of itself.

This is a purely European line of reasoning which shows how much the educated Indian of the present day has become Europeanised in intellect. For what is India's great message to the world—the profound truth of which modern European science is only slowly beginning to recognise, though the Founder of the Christian religion proclaimed the same doctrine nineteen hundred years ago—but the irresistible power of abstract thought, the force of an idea? Thought created the universe, thought rules the world, and thought only is indestructible and eternal. The power of Indian thought has not been extinguished by the Europeanisation of the East: it has been for centuries imperceptibly leavening the materialistic science and philosophy of the West, so that western teachers are now beginning to teach Indians what India has taught them. Matter does not create thought, nor destroy thought: schools and colleges do not create ideals, they are created by the ideals. When Indians begin to think Indianly, the schools and colleges will be Indian. Political institutions do not make a country free; freedom is won by thought alone.

India must wait for a better system of Anglo-Indian education, until Great Britain herself also has one;

for the root of this evil is not in Calcutta, Bombay, Madras and Allahabad, but in Oxford, Cambridge, London and Aberdeen. The reform has already begun in Europe, the axe is at the root of this tree, but it will be many years before the old superstitions, which cling like parasites on national education, are entirely destroyed. In the meantime India must attend to the revival of her own national artistic culture, the foundation of all true education. In the preservation of this, Europe is as much concerned as India herself, for what India preserves of it is a gain to humanity. The knowledge you can get from Europe must be a supplement to, not a substitute for, your own artistic inheritance.

Art, in which is included poetry and music, has always been the foundation of national culture. It was so in ancient Greece, in all mediæval Europe and in India; it is so now in China and Japan. In modern Europe, we teach the letter of Greek culture, but suppress the whole spirit and intention of it. Before we proceed further, therefore, in the discussion of educational method, I think it will be useful to consider what were the actual educational methods of the ancient Greeks, of a European nation pre-eminent for physical fitness and intellectual achievements, whose ideal is commonly held up by modern educationists as the highest in the world. We shall then see how little the Pharisees and Sadducees of modern education observe the spirit of the law which they inscribe on their phylacteries. I will quote from an admirable monograph by Miss C. A. Hutton on Greek Terracotta Statuettes *(The Portfolio,* November 1899).

There were three branches of learning—grammar, music and gymnastics. [Other authorities add drawing.] Until he was fourteen, a boy was principally concerned with the two first-named, but at fourteen he was supposed to have finished his studies in grammar, and it was replaced by gymnastics; to this and music, he chiefly devoted his attention during the last four years of his school life. Grammar comprised reading, writing and a little elementary arithmetic. After three years' instruction, the pupil could usually begin to read the poets; his acquaintance with their works was not, however, postponed until he could read them for himself. The great poets supplied the religious influence in Greek life, and a Greek child learnt by heart passages from Homer and Hesiod, as an English child learns passages from the Bible. These were committed to memory from the oral instruction of the teacher, and we now see why education proceeded at so leisurely a pace. Besides selections from the works of Homer and Hesiod, a Greek boy had to learn the many popular songs, hymns, catches, dirges and choral odes, the knowledge of which constituted a liberal education. Few of these have come down to us, except in quotation, because the greater part of a Greek gentleman's library was housed in his head, and everybody knew them by heart.

Poetry, music, memory-training and physical gymnastics—the cultivation of a sense of perfect rhythm in mind and body, in a religious and perfectly artistic environment—these were the vital forces in the intellectual development of ancient Greece. This is what the greatest of Greek philosophers, whose words I have quoted in a previous chapter, says of the educational effect of the sense of rhythm:

Education in music is of the greatest importance, because by that, the measure and harmony enter in the strongest manner, into the inward part of the soul, and most powerfully affect it, making every one decent if he is properly educated, and the reverse if he is not. And, moreover, because the man who hath here been educated as he ought to be, perceives in the quickest manner whatever workmanship is defective, and whatever execution is unhandsome, or whatever productions are of that kind; and being disgusted in a proper manner, he will praise what is beautiful, rejoicing in it, and receiving it into his soul, be nourished by it, and become a worthy and good man; but whatever is ugly, he will in a proper manner despise and hate, whilst yet he is young, and before he is able to understand reason, and when reason comes, such an one as hath been thus educated will embrace it, recognising it perfectly well from its intimate familiarity with him.

There is a real and close kinship between the true Greek educational ideal and the national culture of India which the present Anglo-Indian educational system, and even that which is now called national, almost completely ignore. Every part of the Greek system has its place in the true national culture of India. The cultivation of the sense of perfect rhythm in mind and body, in a religious and perfectly artistic atmosphere, is just as much the true Indian educational ideal as it was that of ancient Greece. In Japan too, in the present day, poetry, art, music and gymnastics take just the same high place in national culture as they did in ancient Greece; and no one who has studied the psychology of national development can doubt for a moment that her present high position among the nations of the world is as much due to her system of national culture as to the scientific appliances and methods she has adapted from the West.

Art in Japan is not a luxury for the rich, but the basis of national education. The coloured prints for which fancy prices are now paid by European Connoisseurs, made by Hokusai, Hiroshige, and other well-known artists, are the work of men belonging to what are called the artisan classes and were produced at the cheapest rate for the poorer classes only. The popular paintings by Indian artists of the same class, despised and uncomprehended by educated Indians to-day are also highly appreciated by Europeans who know what art is. If you read the works of Lafcadio Hearn you will learn that poetry has done as much for national culture in Japan as it did formerly in Greece, and, until the nineteenth century, in India also. Poetical tournaments are still a favourite form of popular entertainment in Japan, and even among the poorest classes any occasion of domestic importance, either joyful or sad, is marked by poems composed by the people themselves. In the spring mornings in Japan the working classes, the poorest of the poor, and not only the well-to-do, will rise by hundreds to watch the opening of the lotus flowers; the flowering of the plum and cherry trees in the early summer are days of national rejoicing. India need not cease to take delight in beauty, and to have faith in the inspiration of nature which her ancient Ṛṣhis taught, because she has become poor. It is far worse to be poor in spirit than to be poor in worldly goods. Modern science and English education are not sufficient substitutes for art. It will not profit India to gain the whole world and lose her own soul.

Even in England it is barely two centuries since art and music had almost as high a place in national culture as they had in ancient Greece, and there can be little doubt but that before two more centuries have passed they will have again recovered their position in European education, from which they have been ousted by the pedantic bookman and the equally pedantic scientific professor. In the early eighteenth century in England musical instruments were hung up in every public inn for public use, because no one could claim to be considered educated who could not play an improvised accompaniment to a song. Poetical composition was a popular amusement, as it is in Japan to-day. The half-penny newspapers and cheap novels have now taken the place of music and poetry. Cheap literature and cheap science have upset the intellectual balance of Europe for a time, but the laws of nature are not changed by scientific discoveries and mechanical inventions;

principles of intellectual development have not been altered since Plato wrote, and the nations which, adapting methods to modern needs, follow these principles best will come out best in the end.

Art in Europe has declined in the last two centuries because it has ceased to belong to national life and culture. It is beginning to revive, and will continue to do so, in proportion to the success of educational reformers in convincing the national consciousness that art is a real necessity of life. Art in India has been declining for similar reasons, but if India realises in time the intellectual value and educational use of national tradition in art, the renaissance of the East will be greater than the renaissance of the West, for the East has not squandered so recklessly those art traditions, the wisdom of ages, which as much as manuscripts, books and scientific inventions, constitute for all time the true basis of civilisation.

CHAPTER VI

EDUCATIONAL METHODS

It is hardly within the province of a European artist to propound methods of art teaching for Indians, because the right methods are intimately associated with national artistic traditions and are best formulated by Indians who have a thorough understanding of artistic principles. The right grasp of principles is the first essential, and without that both the European and the Indian teacher will go astray. When this is joined to a thorough knowledge of traditional methods, Indians will be able to evolve for themselves a working system suitable for the needs of the present day. The greatest hindrance to intellectual progress is the mechanical brain. Stereotyped thought is not, as is commonly assumed, a peculiar product of eastern educational tradition; it is just as often produced by modern European methods, and by education called scientific.

Hardly anything has yet been done in India to collect detailed information, for educational purposes, of the Indian traditional methods of art teaching and practice. Material of this kind would be invaluable for formulating methods suitable for both general and special education. All such traditional methods are worthy of the attention of educationists, and should be systematised for the purpose of hand-and-eye training and the development of the imaginative faculties in general education. Every Indian household should sedulously keep up traditional art practice, such as that of drawing symbolic designs in rice-powder on the ground in front of the doorway. When they are drawn by hand only, using both right and left without the mechanical aid of stencil plates, this is an inexpensive and excellent method of hand-and-eye training for children of all ages.

Dr. Coomaraswamy, in his book on *Mediæval Sinhalese Art,* has described the traditional method of teaching drawing practised by the craftsmen of Ceylon. He has also collected some of the words, but not the music of the craftsmen's songs. In every part of the world, when art is living and life is healthy, the craftsmen and labourers have always sung at their work; and no great art has ever been created without an accompaniment of song, for art itself is but the music of form and colour. These traditions of art and music belong to the treasury of your national culture, and a system of national education which has no place for them is national only in name. The soul of a people lives in their songs, and national life dies when songs are no longer made and sung. Your treasury has become sadly depleted and it is high time you began to take count of what you have left, to use it to greater advantage and to add to your store. Dr. Coomaraswamy's pioneer work should be supplemented by a systematic survey and record for all India.

There are songs for gladness and songs for sorrow, but it is mostly the songs of gladness which inspire and accompany art creation.

I wrote in a previous chapter that, before art can really revive in India again, the people must be glad; you must drive away the demons of plague and malaria, and instil into the minds of the people those elementary ideas of order, decency and cleanliness which are at the root of all art. In the April 1909 number of the *Modern Review* I read with great pleasure and interest an article on 'Education through Social Helpfulness,' by Professor D. J. Fleming, of the Forman Christian College, Lahore, from which I quote the following typical illustrations of voluntary work done by students of various colleges in different parts of India:

The widespread malaria which followed the heavy rains of the Punjab last summer, gave another opportunity for students. One little band in a single day gave out two hundred packets of quinine obtained from their Municipal Committee, to suffering Bhangars, and three hundred packets in the Dhobi Mandi. This experience, better than any lectures, brought before these men the poverty and suffering of the submerged classes and inspired them with a desire to alleviate their social, moral and physical condition. They found that to make quinine effective they often had to take a little sweeper child in their arms and themselves give the medicine; or to reach the prostrate patient they had to follow their teacher into the house of a village Chamar. More effective than hours of talk on the evils of caste is one such deed. Of another school he says:

The reports are about what men have done. As a result you will find this spirit leading a young Brāhmaṇa student to help an old woman to raise her water-pot to her head, or even to carry it a distance. It led the boys last summer to take out 150 sick people in their boats for the fresh air on those beautiful Cashmere lakes; 400 boys were with difficulty and against opposition taught to swim, which meant constant opportunity for serviceableness in that city of boats. A dozen people were saved from drowning by these boys in one season. During the cholera epidemic the schoolmasters formed themselves into night watchers at five centres in the city so that they might be able to take medicine to the stricken at once, which in cholera is all important. During one week of the past winter the boys rescued from the streets sixty starving donkeys, which were taken to the school premises and there fed. When the owners called for them they had to pay, and their future treatment was checked up by selected boys. By example, teachers led them to see that manual work is not degrading, so that, even though they were sometimes jeered at, the Brāhmaṇa boys of this school were last winter hauling logs for the building of a dispensary, while others were carrying sacks of chaff two miles or more on their backs through the city—all for love. Such education means that they will go from the school with a positive attitude towards dirt and wrong and suffering. They will not relieve their feelings with a pious letter to a newspaper, but will put their own shoulders to the wheel. Nor is this all. There is a Waif and Stray Society to which masters and boys subscribe monthly and thereby pay for the schooling of fifty poor boys, clothe a score, and feed and look after those in real distress. They have forty cases in hand now. There is a Sanitation Committee to help and induce the people to put their houses and yards in a sanitary condition. This is a most important work in a city which is yearly overrun with cholera. The Principal and boys have often joined each other in the cleaning of some streets. A Knight Errant Society aims at the protection and raising up of women. The Knights pledge themselves to do all in their power to prevent girls being married under the age of fourteen.

Such work as this is true education. The spirit of it inspired the great art of Buḍḍhist India : it belongs to and is necessary for art, for it creates the atmosphere in which art lives. It seems to be a sign of "the Spirit of God moving on the face of the waters". But you should not be content with teaching your young men such elements of art. They should have not only a positive attitude towards dirt and wrong, but a positive understanding of, and desire for, beauty in nature and rightness in art. For when the poor have that feeling of beauty and rightness they too will have a positive dislike for dirt and disorder, and will not wait for charity to help them. They will have, moreover, in their own minds a perennial source of joy and consolation which God has given for all His creatures, rich and poor alike.

Though every country has to develop methods of teaching in conformity with its national traditions of culture, it is always useful for educationists to compare notes with similar work in other countries. The Report of the Third International Art Congress, held in London in 1908 under the patronage of H. R. H. the Prince of Wales, affords to Indian educationists many useful suggestions. The Congress itself was a striking proof of the progress which art is making in modern European and American Educational methods. It had a membership of over 1,800 including nearly 200 delegates representing thirty-eight different countries. In the Congress Exhibition the work of twenty-one nations was represented. Two important illustrated reports published in connection with the Congress work are the German one, 'Deutsche Kunst-Erziehung,' edited by Professor Behreus which gives a succinct account of the present state of art education in Germany, and an American one, '*Art Education in the Public Schools of the United States*'. It is significant that two of the most progressive of western nations, Germany and America, are the keenest in interest in art education.

The subject of the papers read at the Congress, and printed in its report, covered a very wide field. I will notice in detail those which convey useful suggestions to Indian educational reformers. A paper by Mr. T. C. Horsfall, President of the

Manchester University Settlement, on methods of disseminating knowledge and love of art, gives a lurid picture of the state of the great industrial cities of Europe, produced by the methods of modern industrialism, the very same methods which are constantly held up for the admiration and imitation of Indians. Mr. Horsfall thus describes the conditions of life in Manchester when his Committee began work in 1877:

The majority of the adult inhabitants did not know that beauty of nature and art is an appearance of rightness which should be found everywhere; they did not even know that beauty of art existed; and the majority of even the well-to-do classes regarded art as a luxury, of which it was desirable to have a little kept here and there in separate buildings, to prove that Manchester could afford, and was intelligent enough to buy, all that the other towns provided themselves with. No attempt was made, or even now is made, to free the air from the smoke of houses, and very little attempt was made to free it from the smoke of mills and works. The air, therefore, was horribly filthy, and cut off the greater part of the light which the feeble Lancashire sun supplied. Although the influence of the town and of most of its industries was remarkably unfavourable to health and strength, no attempt had ever been made to base the whole system of education on good physical training, and it has only been quite recently that a certain amount of such training has been added to a curriculum mainly consisting of the use of letters and signs. No attempt had been made, or has yet been made, to ensure that what art there was in the town should be of the national kind, and those of the buildings which have some beauty are bewildering in their variety of style. There were large districts, covering many square miles, in which nearly all the dwellings, with the exception of public houses (drink-shops) and a few doctor's houses, were the cottages of work people, mostly of the poorer classes, arranged in long monotonous rows. There were a few large parks, but no attempt had been made to bring a planted open space within reach of every group of dwellings. There were no trees in the streets, and the light was too dim and the air too acid to allow plants to flower or their leaves to thrive in the houses. The filthiness of the air prevented women from wearing bright-coloured dresses; there were no beautiful buildings; no beautiful furniture; ignorance of nature and of art had probably there reached a degree of completeness unequalled in any other country. Drunkenness and betting were, of course, extremely common. As no well-to-do people would live in such districts, the poorer classes were more isolated than in any other country. A very trustworthy clergyman told me that ignorance of even the appearance of persons of the well-to-do classes was so great that he had known children cry with fright when he, in his black clothes, entered their courts. In all large towns, where inquiry is made, it is found that most of the children know very little about flowers, trees and birds, but probably nowhere else was so large a proportion of children so ignorant of such things as in Manchester thirty years ago. An Inspector of schools told us that he had found a large class of children in an Ancoats school, not one of whom knew what a bee was like or where it was to be found; and of a class of boys in the sixth standard, in which only four boys out of twenty had ever seen a lark, and of the four, one had only seen a lark in a cage at a public house. Some Manchester children sent for a holiday into the country where I lived, on passing under a mountain-ash tree, asked, respecting a bunch of red berries: "Are them roses?" And I have been asked by a Manchester woman to whom I had talked about squirrels: "And what kind of birds might them be?" And not one of a group of at least a dozen other women smiled at the question.

What a commentary on our boasted western civilisation is the condition of one of the greatest cities in the Empire, a city which is representative of all that 'modern progress' which seems so alluring to many Indian industrial and social reformers! The aim of the Art Museum over which Mr. Horsfall presides, situated in one of the poorest and most crowded districts of Manchester, was to revive and strengthen any knowledge and love of nature which its visitors might bring to it, and to show to those who did not already possess it, the fact that Manchester, with all its hideousness and depravity, lies in a beautiful district. Mr. Horsfall collected the best representations in colour he could get, of the common wild flowers of the district, of common garden flowers, of the birds of the district, and also of flowers and birds which though not found in the district, are often mentioned in books; of all the animals of which the working classes are likely to hear the names, of the common kinds of trees, of their foliage, blossom and fruit; pictures and photographs of places near the city, interesting either for their beauty or for some other reason; pictures of beautiful scenery in other parts of England. In the Museum collections lent to schools, labels of advice were attached to exhibits. A label under pictures of landscape states that love of beauty is necessary for health and happiness, and that some measure of it may be gained by looking carefully at objects in the Museum and by forming the habit of recalling their colours and forms; but visitors were advised, after examining the pictures of local scenery, to go to see the places and to try to enjoy their beauty, and then to enjoy the pictures more fully. To show the visitors that even a small, poor home can be made attractive, a model sitting-room and bedroom, prepared by two distinguished artists for the purpose, was exhibited in the Museum, and, says Mr. Horsfall, no other part of the Museum had more influence for good.

The methods adopted by this Museum Art Committee for contending with the terrible condition of the industrial classes in Manchester are, of course, only palliatives which leave the root of the evil untouched. No museums and art collections, or methods of art teaching can deal effectively with such evils as these, though Mr. Horsfall says that a good deal has been done to brighten the lives of the people. Working men assured him that what they had learnt in the museum had made the world a new and richer place for them.

The level of life of a considerable number of families has certainly been much raised by the Museum; parents and children in many families have felt the influence of its pictures, its concerts, its lectures almost every week during the winter months for many years. When Ancoats children who have visited the Museum are taken into the country, it is found that most of them know by sight and names more trees and flowers than many country children know. We are told that Ancoats children compare very favourably with other Manchester children in manners and conduct. That the influence of the Museum has increased the love of nature seems to be shown by the fact that the Association rents a cottage in Derbyshire, in which a large number spend their week-ends during all the warmer parts of the year. The influence of art has certainly been conducive to good citizenship. I know of no set of working people in Manchester who show so much desire for the improvement of the conditions of life in the town as Associates show.

May Anglo-Indian administrators as well as swaḍeshi politicians take these lessons to heart. But, as Mr. Horsfall says: "Art Museums alone cannot arrest the rapidly progressing deterioration of the inhabitants of our great manufacturing towns." Under such conditions art can only alleviate but not cure. What Indians must take care of is that the methods of industrialism which have produced such terrible intellectual, moral and physical degradation in Europe, shall not be allowed to propagate the same evils in India.

One of the influences which have hastened the decline of Indian art and a very great obstacle to its revival, has been the attitude of the Indian Universities towards art education. When the revision of the curriculum of the Calcutta University was under discussion a few years ago, I succeeded in persuading the Faculty of Arts to pass a resolution, almost unanimously, affirming the principle that art should hot be excluded from the Arts ccurse of the University. It also accepted a proposal I made, as a preliminary to a comprehensive scheme for giving art its proper place in the education of Indian undergraduates, to place art in the same position as science in the Matriculation examination. Both of these resolutions were subsequently ignored by the official committee at Simla which settled the final details of the scheme, and art is now totally excluded from the curriculum of "the largest University in the world". How little Anglo-Indian educationists are in touch with the most progressive thought in western education, was clearly shown at the International Art Congress last year, which passed unanimously a resolution calling for the definite inclusion of art in the University curriculum, as essential for a liberal education. Professor Woodward, one of the delegates from the United States, speaking in support of the Resolution, told how far American Universities had already gone in this direction. "There was a distinct tendency in America to include a College of Art in the University," and in some of the best of them they were already included. Ten or twelve of the Universities have established departments of architecture which are centres of art instruction in the Universities. Fifty-one per cent of the students enrolled in the University of Maine took art or drawing in some form or other, and in three other Universities the proportion was twenty-eight per cent, twenty-six and twenty-one.

The narrowness of the views of Anglo-Indian educationists on this point, are, as I have said, only a reflection of the same spirit in English and Scotch Universities, and India has little to expect of larger views until the barriers of pedantry and exclusiveness have been broken down, not only in Great Britain, but among English-educated Indians, who, having lost touch with their own national culture, yet endeavour to build up a system called national in imitation of the least progressive of western educational systems, just as they also attempt to imitate the least progressive of western industrial institutions.

An English delegate at the Congress, Mr. Hine, the Art master at Harrow School, read a paper in which he put the case clearly :

That a subject so very essential to the development of mind and to the cultivation of taste as drawing should have never, as yet, found a place in the [English] University curriculum constitutes an indictment against the illiberal and narrow scheme of education which the Universities adopt. If the authorities at our Universities understood more fully the character of the aims of the ancient Greeks, about whose languages they know so much, they would realise, as did Pamphilus, the master of Apelles, that one of the first steps in a liberal education is the learning of drawing. Even in the days of Queen Elizabeth, men and women of position were considered to be wanting in education, unless they had some practical acquaintance with the fine arts of architecture, painting and music; and now, in these so-called utilitarian days, when so much stress is laid upon the acquirements of such knowledge as can be used profitably and bring some immediate return in material well-being, surely it is wisdom to train the young in a language which is universal in character, the use of which cultivates their powers of observation, and teaches their hands to express with ease and accuracy the objects and wonders of their environment. Apart from these considerations there lies within us all a capacity for appreciating beautiful things, and a latent desire to express our joy in them, and it is the bounden duty of all educationalists to disimprison these qualities and to enlarge them by careful and sympathetic training. There are subjects in the curricula of schools and Universities to which much time is given, that are much less essential to the development of character than is the subject of drawing. Nearly all professions require of those who pursue them some knowledge of drawing, and in many professions this requirement is becoming more and more insistent.

But the chief point, is that by learning to draw well one gains the power of expressing something of one's own best nature and feeling, which is far more even than the power of accurately recording facts. For if man continues to neglect the cultivation of his æsthetic instincts he remains a lop-sided animal, undeveloped and only partially educated, for no one disputes the contention that the contemplation and understanding of great art elevates character and helps to fulfil God's idea of man, and therefore is truly educative. Art is one of the concrete forms in which a nation or community expresses its degree of spiritual attainment, and its effect upon individual character is to enlarge its sympathies and define its feelings. The careful study of the elements of art enables man to appreciate intelligently its achievements. Art is the olive branch in the hands of Peace, and its gentle sway over the minds of men has done much to eliminate therefrom the instincts of the brute; it may therefore be made a stepping-stone to higher things.

At the Universities, where much spare and dangerously idle time is waiting to be profitably filled up, very definite courses of art study should be open to all, practical lectures and good demonstrations should be given, and honours as well as degrees should be possible of attainment. Architecture, painting and handicrafts should be included in the curriculum, and one or more of these subjects made compulsory in the examinations. Thus a very beautiful side of man's nature would be cultivated, invaluable to the community, uplifting and ennobling to the individual.

Mr. Rawson, a delegate from Cape Colony, said:

In education it is sometimes forgotten that the aim is not attainment, nor learning, but the complete development of all the faculties possessed by human beings.

English Universities and many English schools do not really educate in the truest sense, for they leave undeveloped, or half-developed, some of the highest and most important of the human intellectual faculties—those which the Greek educationists, as I have shown, always endeavoured to develop to the highest possible extent. Even viewing the question from a purely utilitarian standpoint, it is entirely wrong to suppose that the development of these faculties is not just as essential for the engineer, the literary man, the school teacher, the doctor and the judge, as it is for the artist. The artistic faculty is not a special compartment of the brain reserved for exercise by the painter, sculptor or craftsman. It is the faculty by which a man in any profession is enabled to attain to the highest place among his fellows, for it is the synthetical faculty as distinguished from the analytical, the creative and selective faculty which connotes the power of appreciating and attaining to rightness in all work, intellectual or physical. It is the faculty which distinguishes the poet from the common rhymester; the great scientist who discovers some principle or law in nature, from the ordinary investigator who catalogues facts and statistics; the original thinker, from the pedant; the engineer who creates great works, from the mechanician who copies regulation designs; the great judge, from the little judge; the great physician, from the common dispenser of drugs; the painter or sculptor who interprets nature, from the mere recorder of facts.

The aim of attaining to perfect fitness and perfect beauty is not confined to any special order of creation, it is a universal one in nature; and so it is, or should be in man. The man for whom art in some form is not a necessary part of education and life is a man whose intellectual and spiritual powers are stunted and undeveloped.

The whole direction of modern western education has been, until quite recently, towards the development of the analytical or critical powers of the intellect, giving to the synthetical powers a subsidiary or subordinate, instead of the highest place, and putting the mode of expression higher than the idea itself. Thus while the classical scholar's highest attainment is considered to be a fine translation of a Greek author, or an elegant imitation of a Greek poet, the vital principle of classic culture is disregarded, and art becomes an archæological prescription taught like Greek etymology and syntax. The great thinkers, scientists and artists which modern Europe has produced are no proof of the excellence of western pedagogics. Genius finds its way whether the school be good or bad. It is the individualist, and not a system, who has produced whatever is great in modern Europe, just as it has been the individual, with capacity enough to rise above departmentalism, who has done the really valuable work in British Indian administration.

If India is to create a real national University it must not be a rigid and exclusive system: it must neither be an imitation of western institutions nor a mere revival of ancient Indian, but one that is comprehensive enough to embrace all aspects of national culture and tradition, while keeping the doors open, in the true spirit of ancient Hinḍuism, to all modern thought. In such a University artistic methods of teaching would receive the full recognition which is now given to them by the most advanced of western educationists; for art, being a universal language, affords to Indian students the means of developing the imaginative and creative faculties which the present Anglo-Indian system entirely neglects. In Anglo-Indian education, as in the English system, the language itself—the mode of expression is more important than the ideas to be expressed.

The intellectual decadence of India in the last few centuries has been greatly due to the same neglect of the imaginative and creative faculties. Book-learning has taken too important a place in intellectual training. The entire absorption of the highest intellect of the nation in the intricacies of Samskṛṭ grammar, and in the study of Samskṛṭ texts, has developed the critical powers of the mind, but not the constructive and imaginative functions. It has been little gain for India that her attention has now been diverted from Samskṛṭ grammar to English grammar and Samskṛṭ books to English books. What India really requires is the enlargement of the sphere of her highest intellectual activity so that it may again embrace all forms of creative energy, represented by art and industry, as it did in the greatest periods of her history.

No amount of critical acumen will regenerate India so long as the creative functions of the brain remain undeveloped in the most intellectual classes of the community. All the important problems of art and industry are waiting for the best brains of the country to attempt their solution; and until art and industry are regarded as an integral part of national education, from the primary school up to the highest degree of the University, these problems will remain unsolved, and India will remain a blind and helpless follower of empirical European prescriptions.

Proper art teaching in the University courses would afford just the relief which is now most needed, to the intolerable strain imposed upon Indian students by the system of giving all instruction in a foreign language. It would relieve some of the overburdened functions of the student's brain and give energy to those most important ones which are now entirely undeveloped. How many of the best students, both in Europe and in India, do not break down before they have passed through the University, on account of the strain caused by excessive book-work? And again, how many Indian students do not seek unhealthy distraction in political agitation and ruin their careers, just because the narrowness and monotony of the University curriculum afford them no other intellectual distraction?

Though European Universities have not yet, like those in America, given art a definite place in the curriculum, many of them do disseminate good artistic influences through the beautiful environment with which members of the old English Colleges are surrounded. Some of the old halls and chapels of these Colleges, and also some of those at the great public schools, are the most beautiful examples of architecture England has produced. The old College gardens at Oxford and Cambridge are famous for their beauty. It is due to this fine environment, more than anything else, that the graduates of English Universities are, as a rule, much more highly developed æsthetically than are the graduates of Indian Universities in which this aspect of education of ignored, for art education is very largely a question of environment.

And with æsthetic influences, moral influences are inseparably joined. It is significant that the Calcutta Colleges, which are nearly all most hideous barracks placed in a hideous and even filthy environment, are the chief centres in which anarchical doctrines have been propagated in India. I do not think that any psychologist would dispute that the ugliness (which connotes immorality) of the environment and the dreary monotony of the curriculum in the Bengal Colleges have tended largely to propagate the immoral methods of political agitation which find favour with some Bengali students. In the former letter I have quoted Hiouen T'sang's description of the beautiful buildings and surroundings of the famous College of ancient India at Nalaṇḍa. The great Chinese scholar seemed to be hinting at the moral influence of such a beautiful environment when, after his description of the buildings and grounds of the College, he comments on the good behaviour of the students, and adds that no case of deliberate rebellion against the rules had been known in the seven hundred years since the foundation of the College.

Until the great wave of utilitarianism passed over Europe in the nineteenth century, European educationists were as fully aware of the importance of environment in the education of youth, for, before the nineteenth century, the utmost care was taken throughout Europe to provide beautiful buildings and harmonious surroundings for all educational institutions. Mrs. Besant lecturing here a short time ago on 'The deadlock in Religion, Science and Art,' said some wise words which Indian educationists should note:

Very many people, I am afraid, in this and other countries do not realise that beauty is a necessity of daily life for the human being, and when he does not get it he is less man, less woman than he ought to be. It is not a question as to whether you should have a beautiful thing as a luxury; it is a necessity, and it should be the daily bread of life... To kill out the sense of beauty which comes by living in contact with Nature—for Nature is beautiful everywhere, and contact with her beautifies the human face and mind—the killing out of that sense of beauty which grows out of the mountains and rivers and the meadows and the groves, that is a national loss, and spells national decay... The life is poor where there is no beauty, and life itself grows common, vulgar, where beauty is not a dominating force. It is one of the great revelations of God Himself, for beauty lies in perfection of harmony, in exquisiteness of outline, in loveliness of colour, and all these things are characteristics of the Divine Workman whose manifestation is always in beauty while wisdom and power underlie it.

We may feel confident that when Mrs. Besant's great scheme for a National University is realised, art as well as religion will resume its proper place in Indian education.

Anglo-Indian educational reformers have lately endeavoured to apply a remedy for the excessive bookishness of their system by introducing modern theoretical and experimental science into the School and the College curricula. The theoretical part of this teaching only substitutes one book for another; the practical side gives a useful relief from book-work, but as an intellectual exercise it is a mere repetition of the literary course, for it keeps the students' minds fixed upon the same ideas as their language lessons; instead of analysing words and phrases they are analysing gases, liquids, minerals or vegetable forms. It is grammar and syntax over again in a concrete form. Thus the new reformed system, upon which so much discussion has taken place, is only perpetuating the vice of the old, that it left the æsthetic, the synthetical and the creative thought-centres half-developed or undeveloped.

When a true Indian National University is established, it must follow other lines of thought; it must endeavour to bring the mind of India back into the channels it followed in the time of its highest development, to make Indian thought creative and not merely assimilative. No College should be affiliated to the National University in which art and music are not part of the intellectual, moral and religious teaching. Every College building should be designed with taste: it need not be an extravagant building with costly decoration—a building may be beautiful without any decoration whatsoever—but it should be fine and dignified in its proportions and well situated. The grounds attached to it should be ample and laid out with skill: the work of making and keeping the environment of the College beautiful with trees and plants and flowers should not be left entirely to servants and gardeners, but should be a part of the College curriculum. In the College garden students should be brought into touch with some of the beauties of nature, to observe the rhythm of tree growth and plant growth and to watch their development, to reverence beauty as part of the Divine nature, and to create beauty for themselves. Some part of the College buildings, for instance, the walls of the quadrangle or courtyard, should be used by the students for practical exercises in decorative design: in this work as well as in gardening, their creative faculties will be brought into play at the same time as the sense of beauty in form and colour is developed. The College hall or lecture room should be decorated with fine wall-paintings of Indian subjects by Indian artists. Illustrations of the most beautiful examples of Indian art and architecture should be hung upon the walls of the class rooms and form the subject of discussion by the Professors and students.

A part of the time set apart for physical culture should be given to hand-weaving. The movement of the shuttle and of the lay by the hands and arms, and of the treadles by the feet in the process of hand weaving give rhythmic muscular exercises for the arms and legs very similar to those which are now used in the Swedish system of physical culture, a system which is acknowledged to be the best in Europe at the present day. The Swedish system itself is based upon the principles of the old Greek system of physical culture. I do not mean that weaving will give all the movements necessary for proper physical training, but it will be quite easy to supplement the weaving exercises with other muscular movements to make the course complete.

The advantages for India of combining physical culture with hand-weaving are obvious. It would be more interesting for the students than ordinary gymnastic exercises; it would train the eye and hand as well as the muscles of the body; it would teach the students to give due respect to manual occupations, and it would concentrate the highest intellect of the people upon the industrial problems which are of vital importance for national prosperity. It is not that all University students should be prepared for taking up industrial or artistic professions; it is that all should be trained as citizens as well as scholars, as men of action, as well as men who talk and write; they must become more perfect human beings with wider views of life. National education must be based upon the consideration of national needs, which urgently demand a more perfect and complete development of all the nerve centres in Indian youth than that which is given to them now by the Anglo-Indian and British pedagogic systems. The nerve centres which control action must be developed as well as those which control the assimilative and reflective functions of the brain; and they must be trained more thoroughly and scientifically than they are by the present teaching in schools and colleges. There is as much evil in over-literacy as there is in illiteracy, though the Census statistics only take note of the latter. Indian education is now defective from excess of literacy, Indian intellect suffers from wordiness, from ignoring art as a great intellectual and spiritual force, and the reforms hitherto introduced into the University system leave this great evil untouched.

Sir William Richmond, R.A., in a paper read at the Art Congress held in 1911, said:

> The Government can hardly be said to have extended sympathy to what should be national arts: the drama, the graphic arts and literature. There is no other country in Europe where so little money is expended in the cause of the arts generally as in England. The attitude of the Universities of Oxford and Cambridge has been so full of prejudice that they have been slow to answer the demands which relate to the progress of music, the drama, and the graphic arts. It is true that there is a professor of music, a Slade professor of fine art, and a professor of archæology, but the

general tone of the University is rather to accept these subjects as incidental, and perhaps deplore a little, that they are even incidental. So far, excepting in the case of students with a very distinct bias in the direction of such studies, the greater number of the undergraduates leave the Universities as ignorant of the place the arts have occupied in ancient and modern history, as they were when they left school. It is to be doubted if the practical teaching of the graphic arts will ever assume a place proportionate to their value in any University: yet the history of art might be taught as an integral and indispensable part of education, the history of the arts of Egypt, Assyria, Greece, Italy, France and England. It is a truism to state that the history of Egypt would be unknown to us save for its art; that Assyria has given us, through its art, the history of its kings, and to a large extent the history of its civilisation; the place that art took in Greece everybody knows; the influence of the arts on the grandeur of the Italian States can hardly be exaggerated. In France it not only was, but is, considered to be a natural and necessary part of culture; and our own history proves to us, not only by the cathedrals, but elsewhere, that the graphic arts were practised and encouraged in England up to the time of Henry IV, and crafts, bearing as noble a record as those produced in Italy, at the same period and even later.

This bears out what I have said before, that the cause of the inefficiency of Indian Universities must be looked for in Oxford and Cambridge, London and Aberdeen. It is not to be expected that Anglo-Indian educationists will understand art better in India than they do in Europe, nor will Indians find in English and Scotch Universities all that is wanting in the Indian.

CHAPTER VII

INDIAN SCHOOLS OF ART

In a paper read before the Indian section of the Royal Society of Arts a short time ago, Mr. Cecil Burns, Principal of the Bombay School of Art, expounds and defends his views of the right policy for Schools of Art in India, and these views represent fairly accurately the official policy in art administration for the last fifty years. Mr. Burns begins by affirming that "up to the year 1850, India, from an artistic standpoint, was almost entirely isolated from the rest of the world". This isolation, he argues, protected Indian craftsmen from the competition of the rest of the world, and gave them a practical monopoly in the local markets. On account of this isolation and monopoly, the workmen became unambitious; they made no attempt to devise new patterns or to improve their methods, and thus "they lost whatever power of original thinking they may have formerly possessed". The construction of the Suez Canal opened the flood gates of European art upon them when they were thus unprepared and lethargic, and "*India from an artistic point of view quickly became and has since remained a suburb of Paris and London, as she is from an industrial point of view the suburb of Manchester and Birmingham. . . . The ancient craftwork of India is as dead as the art of the Greeks or as that of the Renaissance in Europe."*

Just as many Europeans, when they talk of the civilisation of the world, mean the civilisation of the particular corner of Europe with which they are most familiar, so Mr. Burns writes of 'Indian art' when he means so much of it as has come under his observation. None of the illustrations he gave of the incapacity of modern Indian craftsmen—of ornamental jars that will not hold water, incongruous teapots, wedding presents, etc.—belong to true Indian art, but to the insignificant and unworthy part of it which enters into Anglo-Indian life, or into the social life of the small section of the Indian people who substitute Anglo-Indian fashions for art. But Bombay is not India, and Anglo-Indian fashions do not as yet dominate all Indian art, or even the most important part of it. If India is now artistically a suburb of Paris and London, then Indian art is dead, and all I have been writing about the living art of India is nonsense. If Indian art is dead, then Indian religion is dead; for Indian art has always been religious art, and when it is no longer so, it will cease to be Indian art. If Indian art is dead, then Indian civilisation is dead, and India itself is a mere geographical expression. Those high ideals which Indians are now striving after are limited by the intellectual horizon of suburban London and Paris.

But Indian art is not dead. Before I went out to India, twenty-five years ago, one of my official predecessors at the Madras School of Arts told me exactly the same thing of Madras as Mr. Burns is now telling of Bombay—that Madras was "artistically a desert". Yet when I came there and began to organise the School of Arts as a craft-school I had no difficulty in finding in a very short time three exceedingly fine Madrasi craftsmen to place in charge of the three departments of craft teaching which I wished to develop. One was a skilled wood carver from Ramnad; another a temple metal worker, a *stapathi,* from Kumbakonam; and the third a goldsmith from the Vizagapatam district. All three were not only very fine craftsmen and designers, who would have commanded very high wages in London or Paris, but they were excellent teachers, knowing their Silpa-Sāsṭras, and artists who were perfectly well able to adapt their designs to any new idea I suggested to them. It was a real artistic delight to work with such craftsmen as these. But when I left Madras it was thought desirable to convert the school into a manufactory for aluminium cooking pots, and Indian art again became invisible to official eyes. I have had the same experience many times since. I have been repeatedly told by official experts that

Indian art is dead, and have always found it very much alive in the places where they declared it to be non-existent.

Mr. Burns, as a good man struggling with adversity, deserves commiseration in his attempt to explain to official satisfaction the decadence of Indian art, and no doubt he will get his due meed of sympathy from the gods on Olympus, but I fear that Indian art will not gain much from his present ideas of the functions of Schools of Art in India. The Suez Canal has been used many times before as a convenient explanation for departmental shortcomings in art administration, and it is really surprising that it is not more frequently blocked in consequence of the things which are thus dumped into it. Indian craftsmen were not more isolated from the rest of the world before the opening of the Suez Canal than were their fellow-workers in Europe before the introduction of railways and steamships. Craftsmanship in Europe has not been improved by the greater facilities of communication and by the application of steam and electric power; it has enormously deteriorated, and the institution of schools of art and craft in Europe was the official recognition of the fact which was forcibly impressed upon the English Government by the Report of the Great Exhibition of 1857 in London. Before the opening of the Suez Canal, Indian craftsmanship had not deteriorated to anything like the same extent as had craftsmanship in Great Britain; so when the

Government opened Schools of Art in India fifty years ago, and placed them under European supervision, they were trying to teach things which the best Indian craftsman knew better than the European. If in the last fifty years Indian craftsmanship has become "as dead as the art of the Greeks," that fact alone is the most damning evidence of the inefficiency of our art administration in India that could be brought forward.

What Indian craftsmanship has suffered from is not the competition of European art, because, as every artist knows, the best European art is never seen in India; it is, that, through the Anglo-Indian educational system, public taste in India has enormously deteriorated, and the high artistic standard of Indian public works in times anterior to British rule has been lowered to the level of suburban London and Paris, through the entire absence of artistic training in Public Works officers of all grades. The Public Works officers have not been able to make proper use of Indian art, because, except as it were by accident, they do not know any art; and English-educated Indians have tried to reproduce suburban England in India because they too, being ignorant of art, have no artistic discrimination and only wish to follow official fashions. It requires great artistic knowledge to be able to adapt the religious art and architecture of India to secular purposes. The Moguls succeeded in doing this admirably, because they brought with them trained craftsmen who were willing to learn from the splendid Hinḍū craftsmen whom they employed in their public works. The Moguls allowed the Hinḍū craftsmen, who were more skilled than themselves, to carry out their artistic ideas for them, and thus Indian art, stimulated by the new ideas, expanded and developed under the Mogul system. Our Public Works administration has never been willing to learn from Indian craftsmen. It insists upon lowering the standard of public taste in India to the level of its own artistic inefficiency by forcing upon the craftsmen, not English art, but English suburbanism.

Mr. Burns rightly points out that the task given to the Schools of Art has been, in the position in which they are placed, an utterly impossible one. "They have had to struggle through periods of alternate neglect and encouragement, according to the individual tastes of succeeding Governors and Lieutenant-Governors, not to mention Directors of Public Instruction, which made continuous development impossible." But he avoids the root of the matter by omitting to add that the work of Schools of Art will always be futile so long as the principles they are supposed to teach are utterly disregarded by the Education Department, the Public Works Department and every other department of the State, as they are now.

Mr. Burns, in reply to my comments, objects to my regarding as the keynote of his lecture the sentence "that although the artistic capacity of the Indian people is still present, the ancient craftwork of India is as dead as that of the Greeks, or of the Renaissance in Europe". I will, therefore, amend my statement and take Mr. Burns' own version of his text which is "that we have in the past attempted to carry out our theories of what Indian art might be, regardless of the changed conditions of the country, instead of making those conditions the basis of our theories".

In that case everything depends upon the correct diagnosis of those conditions, and here Mr. Burns and myself hold diametrically opposite views. Mr. Burns believes that Indian craftsmanship is dead, and that India is artistically a suburb of London and Paris. I agree entirely with Sir George Birdwood, who took part in the discussion, when he said:

> Indian craftsmen are to this day, intrinsically, in every respect, capable of sustaining their reputation of the past in its greatest periods; any default in their traditionary inspiration and manipulative sleights being observable only where the opportunities for their free and untrammelled exercise are closed to them by the overwhelming competitions of Europe and America; and in an insignificant and utterly negligible proportion, our Schools of Art, where these have been, from time to time, degraded from their higher objects, and debased to the status of commercial factories, for the purpose of providing an income out of the penurious pocket of the personally conducted 'globe-trotter,' in part repayment of the costs of their maintenance by the State.

Sir George Birdwood has not been in India for thirty years, but I am able from my recent experience on the spot to endorse every word of this, though I will not go so far as Sir George in saying that the sumptuary industries "such as embroidery in gold and silver and jewellery, still flourish as healthfully and serenely, and in as superb and supreme beauty and glory, as ever under the greatest of the Mogul Emperors of Delhi". It is not, unfortunately, true that they show no signs of decay in their technique or their artistry; but the vital strength of Indian handicraft is still so great that with a better understanding of art on the part of educated Indians, and better administrative methods on the part of Government there is every reason to believe that it would soon recover all that it has lost.

If, as Mr. Cecil Burns affirms, Indian craftsmanship is dead, it is certainly strange that during the last twenty or thirty years European manufacturers have devoted a great deal of attention to investigating the methods of the Indian craftsman, and in many cases applied these methods to the improvement of European industry. In a previous chapter I gave an instance of a purely Indian handicraft being introduced into Holland, Germany and Italy, in which the traditional technique of the Indian craftsman was applied to European industry, without any modification or improvement, in order to produce more valuable and more artistic work than can be produced by the usual modern European commercial processes. This has been the principle on which the best European manufacturers have worked in their exploitation of the Indian craftsman's traditional technique, and it is a thoroughly sound principle both artistically and commercially. It is a thoroughly unsound principle, which is being adopted in India, to reverse this principle and tell the Indian craftsman to adopt the inferior commercial European processes, only for the purpose of competing with the lower class of European manufactures.

If Mr. Burns has, as he says, faith in the power of the Indian people to take the high place they formerly held in the world of art, and to make that place a reflection of Indian ideals and character, he must not accept as inevitable and permanent the degradation of Indian ideals to the level of commercial Europe. The ideals of suburban London will not restore Indian art to its former greatness. It is unfortunately true, as Dr. Coomaraswamy says, that the majority of English-educated Indians who call themselves nationalists do not really love India—they love suburban England, and the comfortable bourgeois prosperity that they hope will one day be established, when India has learned enough science and forgotten enough art to successfully compete with Europe in a commercial war conducted on European lines—but India, at heart, still remains true to herself, and England's highest ideals are not the ideals of suburban

London. There are already unmistakable signs in India of a reaction against the tendency which Mr. Burns would regard as a permanent condition of Indian life instead of a passing phase, a turn in the upward spiral of India's progress. In all stages of human progress it is not the ideals of the majority, but the ideals of the few, which lead the way; and there are a few Indians who are now showing the way in art.

But Mr. Burns will have nothing to do with 'theorists' and 'idealists;' he says we must be practical—follow the crowd, not lead it —we must recognise the present condition of things as inevitable and permanent and adapt our administrative policy to these conditions. In other words we must let the degraded artistic standard of modern Indian life govern our artistic policy, accept the preference of the majority of educated Indians for the art of suburban London and Paris as the dominating factor, and throw over Indian artistic traditions as worn out and useless. We must teach Indian students, he says, sound principles in design by taking them back to nature, "and then make them thorough and expert craftsmen and so arm them for the battle of life". The suggestion that Indian art and craft are only suffering from ignorance of the principles of design and neglect of the study of nature, is to me an amazing one, and shows that Mr. Burns has yet a great deal to learn of Indian art outside the environment of Anglo-Indian life.

I have never disputed that the ancient craftwork of India is exhibiting signs of decay, but I do dispute most emphatically the efficacy of Mr. Burns' prescriptions. Indian craftsmanship has deteriorated, but why? Not from the craftsman's neglect of principles of design, nor from ignorance of nature, but because the good Indian craftsman is unable to find remunerative employment. And why has the demand for his best work diminished? Because the national artistic standard of India has been lowered. The wise physician will surely try to devise means for restoring the artistic standard, and thus drive out the disease; and the best way of doing this, as far as Government is concerned, is by restoring to the good Indian craftsman the opportunities for employment in Government service which are now denied to him. It is only adding insult to injury to preach to him principles of art (which no one knows better than he how to practise) so long as our educational and public works systems continue to dishonour all Indian artists and craftsmen and to keep them out of employment by neglecting the very principles which we preach in Schools of Art.

Mr. Burns' further charge against the Indian craftsman—that he is illiterate—was sufficiently answered by Sir George Birdwood.

They are as found in the village communities of western India, the most literary peasantry in the world, not excepting those of France and Scotland (which received most of its 'culture' from France and Switzerland) and spend all their evenings in the rapt enjoyment of recitations from their great national epics, the *Rāmāyaṇa* and *Māhābhāraṭa* and the religious and patriotic poems of Ṭukarām. It is as if our agriculturists and artisans spent their evenings around our parish churches and on our village greens, in popular readings from Shakespeare, Milton and Swinburne.

What India wants is less 'literacy' of the European kind, and more art. Heaven preserve Indian artists and craftsmen from the literacy of our Anglo-Indian schools and colleges.

I will deal now with the methods of teaching followed in the Bombay school. First, with regard to the teaching of drawing and design, Mr. Burns obviously puts into practice his theory that Indian craftsmanship is dead and buried. Works executed by students in the design classes of the Bombay School of Art, and drawing classes of the High Schools of Bombay were exhibited in the lecture room—works which, as Mr. Burns pointed out, showed extraordinary facility when compared with the same kind of work done by European boys of similar age. The great aptitude of Indian students for ornamental design is familiar to anyone with experience of art teaching in India. But the great fault of these drawings and designs, to my mind, was that, if they had not been labelled 'Bombay School of Art,' no one could have suspected that they were the work of Indian students. They were of exactly the same character, the same treatment of nature, the same method of design, as the drawings and designs from English Schools of Art which for several weeks past have come under my observation as an Art Examiner for the Board of Education in London. The designs were in no sense Indian designs, for Indian ideas of art did not enter into them; they were all clever adaptations, or translations, of modern English ideas. Now the great value of art in general education is that it helps to develop the imaginative faculties, the inborn and intuitive powers of thinking. But in a system by which Indian students are taken away from their national intellectual environment and placed in an artificial one created by a foreign teacher, they are only exercising their original powers of thinking to a very limited extent; they are for the most part assimilating the thought of the teacher. Their brains are becoming not creative, but mechanical. Their art, so far as it is art, is only imitative. India by this process of teaching is becoming a suburb of London and Paris.

Mr. Burns seems to make the mistake, which so many European artists have made in India, of introducing a modern European formula of art teaching, in the belief that it represents fundamental principles governing all art creation. Nature, indeed, is as he maintains, the fountain-head of art: but he is mistaken in supposing that the Indian craftsman in following his tradition has lost touch with nature. Mr. Burns has not yet realised that the Indian craftsman looks at nature with different eyes from his; that Indian art gives a different interpretation of nature from that of modern Europe, and that Indian Schools of Art which substitute the modern European philosophy or grammar of art for that of India are, by a subtle and insidious process, destroying Indian art root and branch. Let Indian artists and craftsmen by all means always go to nature for fresh inspiration; but once they are taught to look at nature through European spectacles, and not in the light of Indian tradition, they cease to be Indian artists and craftsmen.

For Indians to found their art upon tradition does not necessarily mean, as Mr. Burns argued, that "they let their ancestors do their thinking for them". Mr. Lewis F. Day stated the case correctly when he said that tradition was really the sum of all experience. It was tradition that had brought Indian art to the perfection it had once reached, and all advancement in art started from it. Even if Indian art were as debased as Mr. Burns said it was, the starting point should still be tradition. I will come now to Mr. Burns' proposals for extending the practical work of Schools of Art. These were that Government should establish a drawing office and studio, with a certain number of workshops, in which the best decorative work to be placed in public buildings should be designed and made. He suggested that the whole establishment should be under the control of a small Board consisting of the Consulting Architect to Government, an Engineer or Accounts Officer of the Public Works Department, and the Principal of the School of Art, and that it should be run on purely business lines. It is difficult to see in this proposition where Indian art comes in. The principle of using the Schools of Art to co-operate in the design, and decoration of Public Works in India is one which I have consistently advocated for the last twenty-five years, but Mr. Burns hardly alludes to the difficulties which in present circumstances, make such co-operation totally ineffective for the good of Indian art.

The chief one is that the Public Works Department has, with rare exceptions, ever since it was instituted, adopted European, or *quasi*-European styles of architecture for the design of all public buildings in India. Mr. Burns was constrained to admit the force of what I have always contended—that, as all the principal decorative arts have originated from and are dependent upon architectural style, this policy must govern the whole situation with regard to official artistic influence in India—but nevertheless he was willing to accept the Public Works policy which is necessarily extremely detrimental to Indian art and craft, as another inevitable sequence of the opening of the Suez Canal, and contented himself with the observation that "the arguments for and against the adoption of European styles in modern Indian buildings were ably stated in a paper read before this Society by Mr. T. R. Smith in 1873, and the question has since been fully considered in connection with the erection of the Queen Victoria Memorial building in Calcutta".

I must confess that this was entirely new information for me. I have been arguing this point for many years past, but I have remained all this time in ignorance of Mr. Roger Smith's views, and, though I was the senior official art advisor to Government when the scheme for the Victoria Memorial in Calcutta originated, I did not know before that the question had been fully considered in connection with that somewhat unfortunate project. So I hastened to dig up Mr. Roger Smith's paper from the archives of the Royal Society of Arts and I found in it the following:

> The second reason for employing the styles of the country, *viz.*, that the natives can design and build in them, is answered by the fact *that the natives will not be employed.* (The italics are mine.) The buildings which are built for European use and with European funds in India have been invariably built under European superintendence, and from European designs and always will be—and though the artificers may be natives, that does not make the buildings native works, any more than the printing in Calcutta of an English book by Hiṇḍū compositors and pressmen makes it a Hiṇḍū book.

If Mr. Roger Smith is to settle this question for us, we really ought to ask him how he intends to deal with buildings in India which are *not* made exclusively for European use and *not* built exclusively with European funds? Must they, too, always be designed under European superintendence, and must we always consider Indians as rendered permanently unfit for this work by the opening of the Suez Canal? The point seems to me an important one, because I do not know of any public building in India constructed exclusively for European use and built exclusively with European funds. Certainly the Victoria Memorial in Calcutta does not come within this category. Surely Mr. Burns should have left arguments of this kind to moulder peacefully on the bookshelves of the Royal Society of Arts, for they are long since out of date and never represented the best traditions of British administration in India.

However, Mr. Roger Smith admits the possibility of an alternative.

> The designs of these buildings may, it is said, be furnished in the native style (*sic*) by European architects of skill; but I beg very respectfully, but most decidedly, to express my doubt as to the possibility of such a feat being often accomplished satisfactorily.

Why the feat of adapting living Indian styles to public buildings in India should also be left entirely to European architects, Mr. Roger Smith does not attempt to explain; but he certainly estimates the capacity of European architects unnecessarily low, for the feat has been accomplished a good many times since 1873, with results quite as satisfactory as those which have followed the attempts to adapt the archæological styles of Europe to modern requirements in India.

Mr. Roger Smith proceeded to argue that if we had a distinctive, living, national style of architecture in England, we ought unquestionably to use it in our colonies (meaning India) as Rome did in hers, with such changes as local circumstances made necessary. Yes, if we had a living English traditional art to graft on to the living Indian art, a new living art would be developed in which the best elements of both would be united, just as has repeatedly occurred in the art history of nations. But as we have no living traditions to plant in India, Mr. Roger Smith argued in this way:

> There are in existence familiar European styles (archæological styles) well suited to the purpose, and it appears only reasonable that as our administration exhibits European justice, order, law, energy and honour—and that in no hesitating or feeble way—so our buildings ought to hold up a high standard of European art.

There would be some force in the argument if the only principle of British administration in India, were to hold up the virtues of the British nation for the admiration of Indians, regardless of the interests of Indian art and industry. But as it is obvious that the policy which Mr. Roger Smith defended and Mr. Cecil Burns accepts as inevitable is most injurious to both; it seems to me that we should exhibit our virtues in a better light if we did as the Moguls did and employed Indian architects to construct Indian buildings in the styles evolved by Indian conditions, styles which they have always modified to suit changing circumstances and changing ideas, as a living art always is modified. If we have no living architectural style to teach Indians, the only rational and just alternative is to accept the living architectural styles of India and adapt them to our administrative necessities.

Mr. Burns, besides citing Mr. Roger Smith's paper, declared that the question had been fully considered in connection with the project for the Queen Victoria Memorial in Calcutta. I can only give this statement an emphatic contradiction. I myself proposed to Lord Curzon that, as a preliminary to the making of a design for that building, a survey should be made by a competent architect, of living Indian architecture, *i.e.*, of buildings constructed in Indian styles by Indian master-builders who are still alive; that the design for the Memorial should be made in consultation with the best men that were found, and carried out in co-operation with them. Such a survey would have completely disproved Mr. Burns' extraordinary assertion, on which he would base the whole future policy of Schools of Art, that Indian handicraft is dead; and had the Memorial been carried out on those lines the building alone would have justified the scheme.

by giving a splendid encouragement to Indian master-builders, and making a new epoch in Indian art and craft. To my great disappointment Lord Curzon did not see fit to adopt my proposal, on the ground that Calcutta was a European city and that an Indian style would be inappropriate for the building. Sir William Emerson, the architect selected to carry out the design in accordance with Lord Curzon's wishes, did attempt at a public meeting to explain, on architectural grounds, why an Indian style could not be adopted. His argument was, that, with Indian methods of roof construction it was impossible to get the area of open floor space requisite for the large Museum. If this were true, nothing would be simpler than to adapt modern European methods of construction to an Indian design. But as a matter of fact it is altogether a mis-statement. The architects of Bijapur, who invented the ingenious and beautiful method of balancing the weight of a dome inside a building, instead of outside, constructed buildings with an open floor space greater than that of the Pantheon at Rome; and Fergusson, a most competent authority, in describing the tomb of Mahmud as a "wonder of constructive skill," says: "In the Pantheon and most European domes a great mass of masonry is thrown upon the haunches, which entirely hides the external forms and is a singular, clumsy expedient in every respect compared with the elegant mode of hanging the weight inside." Throughout his *History of Indian Architecture* he bears testimony to the constructive ability of modern Indian architects, and shows that Indian architects have always done with Indian architectural styles what all good architects should do—they have adapted them to the requirements of their own times. If European architects are unable to do this it is not the fault of Indian architecture.

Sir William Emerson in endeavouring to defend Lord Curzon's choice of a European style for the Victoria Memorial is entirely inconsistent, for, in 1873, in the discussion on Mr. Roger Smith's paper at the Society of Arts, he differed from the argument of the latter "that the conqueror should carry into the conquered nation a new style of architecture". He declared then:

> The course pursued by the Muhammedans was infinitely preferable. They adapted their architecture to that of the conquered country: European architecture would scarcely suit the requirements of the country. Indeed it is impossible for the architecture of the West to be suitable for the natives of the East and the Muhammedan buildings were found to work well.

I must leave it to my readers to judge how far the facts and arguments bear out Mr. Cecil Burns' statement that the question of adopting an Indian or European style in public buildings was fully considered in connection with the Victoria Memorial at Calcutta. The survey of living Indian architecture which I proposed to Lord Curzon is still an almost indispensable preliminary to any comprehensive scheme for reviving Indian craft. It would be a very easy matter if India had industrial and artistic leaders as numerous and competent as her political spokesmen and writers, but all the Swaḍeshi talking and writing will not lift Indian art out of the mire, and if India is content to become "a suburb of London and Paris," artistically and economically, Government cannot be blamed for not taking the initiative in such things.

It is quite useless for Government Schools of Art to endeavour to encourage Indian art and to propose co-operation with the Public Works Department in the decoration of public buildings, so long as that Department discourages Indian art by setting a higher value upon European decoration, whether it be good or bad. I gave an instance of this in the discussion which took place on Mr. Burns' lecture. There are in Orissa at the present time, within easy reach of Calcutta, a number of first rate Indian craftsmen, masons and stone-carvers, who can execute architectural sculpture vastly superior, not only to Public Works decoration, but to the average work of the same kind produced in any part of Europe in the present day. It can fairly be compared with some of the best Gothic sculpture of the Middle Ages in Europe. Though their present average wages are only four annas a day, the craftsmen are unable to obtain employment, except in the most trivial kind of artistic work, on account of the architectural policy of the Public Works Department. Yet in the Military Secretariat buildings recently erected in Calcutta, and designed as usual in imitation of the Italian Renaissance architecture, masons and stone-carvers were paid at the rate of two rupees a day, only for copying the regulation European ornament prescribed by the European architect. For other buildings in Calcutta and elsewhere a highly paid European sculptor was brought specially from England to provide the architectural decoration; and for the Victoria Memorial very large commissions will be given to European sculptors, as the whole design of the building is European. Over a lac and a half of rupees has been already paid as commission to the European architect. Thus large sums of public money, or moneys chiefly subscribed by Indians, are continually being squandered to the discouragement of Indian art, while large sums are being spent in maintaining Schools of Art for its encouragement. The influence of a single School of Art, however well conducted it may be, is infinitesimal compared with the influence of a great department like that of the Public Works. Either we should cease to pretend to encourage Indian Art; or the architectural policy of the Public Works Department should be made consistent with the fundamental principles of British Indian administration and the avowed objects of the Schools of Art, as they have been defined in the

Despatches of the Secretary of State. The present state of things is wholly irrational, and cannot be justified on political, artistic, or moral grounds.

Since it is generally agreed that the Moguls were eminently successful in their artistic and architectural policy in India, it will be useful to consider the principles on which they worked. Akbar, undoubtedly one of the greatest and most successful of Indian administrators, worked on a very simple principle. He was not a learned man, so he tried to learn from everybody, not to teach what he did not understand. He did not find the Hindū craftsmen too 'illiterate,' because, though illiterate himself, he could appreciate their artistic skill. He took Indian art as he found it, and made the best possible use of it. The Moguls were not an artistic race; a few generations before Akbar they were barbarians whose artistic ideas were limited to pyramids of human skulls. But they had an infinite capacity for assimilating the arts and crafts and the culture of the races which became subject to them. In this respect they resembled the Romans much more closely than we do. Coming into India with the very few and simple architectural ideas which they had learnt in Persia and Central Asia, they found the Hindū builders much superior to their own, and they were not too proud to make use of them. The Hindū craftsmen, on the other hand, being given ample opportunity for exercising their craftsmanship, soon adapted their traditional styles to the requirements and taste of their rulers, and Indian art commenced a new and most vigorous development. It is a common mistake of European writers to attribute that development to Muhammedan artistic genius. It was rather due to the sensible policy Akbar initiated of utilising the skill of Hindū architects and craftsmen, and to the capacity which the latter showed for improving upon the ideas introduced by the Moguls.

The only reason why our Anglo-Indian administration has been such an artistic failure is that we pursue a diametrically opposite policy, which is artistically unsound and economically extravagant. Nothing could be more extravagant than to waste all the artistic resources of India in the way we are doing now. Certainly with regard to Public Works, Akbar's administration was less extravagant than our own. When the Anglo-Indian Public Works Department was established, instead of employing Indian master-builders, as Akbar did, all important architectural work was put into the hands of European Military or Civil Engineers, some of whom had no previous knowledge of building construction, with the result that a costly building sometimes collapsed as soon as it was put up, from glaring faults in the original design. It thus became imperative to adopt in public buildings a style of architecture which presented the least difficulty to these amateur architects, and the 'classic' European style, being the most simple and constructionally primitive, and thus the most adaptable to the calculations of the departmental budget, became the traditional style of our Public Works architecture.

It has always been popular with amateur architects in Europe for the same reason—it was the easiest to learn. Until a few years ago, membership of the Royal Institute of British Architects could be obtained without passing any examination, and even now anyone can practise as an architect in England without passing any test or obtaining any degree. The 'classic' style is popular with European and Indian contractors for the same reason, that it is the easiest to estimate for and the easiest to build with. It is equally popular with the professors and students of Indian Engineering Colleges, where architecture is treated in the same way as it has been in England; it is an architectural formula which can be taught from diagrams and learnt by heart in a few weeks, so that engineering graduates may pose as architectural designers. The untrained students of Engineering Colleges thus supplant the 'illiterate' Indian master-builders by whose skill the Moguls achieved the greatest of their architectural triumphs.

This inefficiency and stupidity were in no way connected with the opening of the Suez Canal; they were the direct outcome of the system of 'classical' education, which is also largely responsible for the degradation of national art in England. The best modern artistic thought of England is not reflected in such a policy—it is entirely opposed to it. India has a right to expect of us the best that we can give—that which is best for India. There is no reason whatever why our Public Works administration should not be as artistically successful as that of the Moguls, if we followed their efficient artistic methods. But so long as we hold to the principle that none but European architects or untrained literates of the Indian Engineering Colleges shall be employed in the design of public buildings, and that none but European artists shall be placed in charge of Indian Schools of Art, our architectural and artistic policy will never be so perfectly adapted to Indian conditions as that of the Moguls. Indian art and architecture can never be properly practised or taught except by Indians, or by Europeans taught by Indians, and if it be true that the Indian Education Department cannot now, after fifty years, produce Indian architects and artists fully qualified for such appointments, there could be no more convincing proof of the unsoundness of our artistic methods.

The proper function of Indian Schools of Art now is to help to repair the blunders of fifty years' inefficient educational administration, and thus to prepare the way for an efficient system of Public Works, established on a sound artistic foundation instead of on academic sophistry, archæological prejudices and departmental incompetence. The weakness of the policy outlined by Mr. Cecil Burns in his paper is due to his failure to understand the psychological conditions in India of the present day. He admits, that, if Indian art is to really revive, the movement must come from within, and in that case it will revive whether the official policy is right or wrong. But he cannot see the signs of the times, or feel that the growth of the Indian national consciousness, which is now going on apace, will surely make and is already making itself manifest in an artistic revival which is a reaction and a protest against the continued denationalisation of Indian art. For Government to ignore that protest, as Mr. Burns advises by accepting the departmental *status quo* as inevitable and unchangeable, is political folly. By doing so the coming artistic renaissance will grow to be an anti-British movement, a visible sign of an ever increasing cleavage between the rulers and the ruled. By adopting a more far-seeing, a more just and more artistic policy, Government would rally round it all the best elements of national feeling. By learning to understand and make better use of Indian art, Indians and Europeans might learn to understand each other better, and to overcome their mutual, racial, religious and political differences. The impetus which Government might give to Indian art by a thorough reform of departmental machinery would open up many new avenues of employment to Indian youths, and thus remove one of the principal causes of the present unrest; but the half measures which Mr. Burns proposes lead nowhere except to set up a permanent barrier between Europeans and the more enlightened of the non-official Indians.

CHAPTER VIII

THE EDUCATION OF THE CHILD

HAVING discussed art in its relation to University and school education, and to special work of Schools of Art, I come now to the education of the child. In many ways this is for Indians by far the most important section of the subject, because it relates to those early years of childhood when the teaching and influence of the parents shape the whole temperament and character of the future man or woman. It is in the home, rather than in the school, or University, or Council Chamber, that the whole foundation of India's artistic and industrial regeneration, as well as the foundation of her political self-government, must be laid. The ideals of each individual householder make the ideals of the nation: the demands of the household construct the whole fabric of national art and industry. National art is formed upon national character; if the Indian household is denationalised, Indian art will become so and the political 'freedom' which is the ideal of the educated Indian, will not make it otherwise.

The Report of the International Art Congress, to which I have referred before, gives many suggestions to Indian parents on infant education. Several of the most important papers were on the teaching of drawing in Infant Schools, and one of the most interesting sections of the Congress Exhibition was a collection of drawings sent from the London County Council Infant Schools. This is a part of a child's education which any intelligent Indian parent can direct in his own home. One of the most instructive Art Exhibitions in London is the annual Exhibition of the Royal Drawing Society, in which drawings by infants beginning at the age of two and a half years are shown. Just as in the earliest ages of humanity, before written language was fully developed, so even now the inchoate scrawlings of childhood represent its first attempts to give ideas visible form, and the best educationists in Europe recognise that this infantile scribbling may be used as a means of developing the child intelligence.

At the Art Congress, Mr. Dow, Professor of Fine Art in the Teachers' College, Columbia University, declared:

> That art teachers had before them the task of convincing the public that art education furnishes *the finest* kind of training for children. Inadequate teaching is responsible for the misconceptions of the public mind as to the significance of art. If the nature of fine arts were better understood, art training would be recognised as an indispensable part of education.

Mr. Ebenezer Cooke, delegate from the Teachers' Guild, London, read an excellent paper on experiments in the teaching of young children, in which he emphasised the importance of drawing.

It not only stimulates observation, deepens impressions, and helps to form clear ideas, but it is also a means of expression and verification. Speech helps the process of thought *but drawing helps to form the ideas themselves* .... Children draw from their own ideas for play. The teacher should take advantage of this, and play at drawing. Each child might name an object in the room, field, or garden, an animal or bird, and let all draw it from their own knowledge and then look at it. Children draw from memory and imagination. Adopt this. Show them an object for a minute or longer, take it away, and draw it from memory. Repeat the drawing after a day, a week, or later. Illustrate a nursery rhyme, a verse of poetry, a story or fairy tale. The figures children make are their own, but there is a law in their development. To improve them, appeal to facts and to knowledge. The man has no arms. Why not? When the drawings are done put them before the class. The backward children will learn from the more advanced. It is often said: "Give childern only the best work." If we give the head of Apollo or Athene to a child it will be treated in the child's own archaic manner. We cannot alter development; we must recognise it. Let no conscious weakness prevent any one from attempting the human figure from imagination. Begin with the child's own figures. Help the child by working with its own knowledge; both what it wants to express and its knowledge of form, the means of expression also. Begin at the known; give colour, and use the brush to draw with or without line. Shape or model the colour into form while it is wet at its edges. Invent patterns with lines, forms, and colours to provide knowledge, and to give facility with the means of expression.

These are practical suggestions which can easily be adapted to Indian conditions, especially if the parent seeks the help of a wood carver, cotton printer or a painter employed in temple decoration, or any other craftsman practising the traditions of Indian art, so that the teaching may have a true Indian character. Miss Katherine Phillips, Superintendent of Method for the London County Council, gave some explanations of the teaching in the Council's Infant Schools.

The drawing of little children is recognised by our teachers to be a language—another means of expression for the developing, struggling, child intelligence. In our good modern infants' schools the little children are now not only allowed, but *required to see for themselves,* and required to record *their own* observations and impressions, or ideas of *their* observations and impressions, not what an outside adult authority insists to them is there to be seen. . . . In this work little children are not now separated from life—the real stirring actual life about them. How truly this is everywhere full of beauty, even among the most ungracious social surroundings, is scarcely realised by those who have never been awakened to 'see' for themselves. If there is nothing else, in some spot of earth desecrated by all foulness and ugliness, there is the sky above, the fruit and vegetables on the coster's barrow, perhaps dray-horses with their fine form and action, and the little children themselves. Little children, through their drawing, are now required, not to postpone living, to some future adult period, but to live fully now, and, through 'seeing,' to learn to love and enjoy the beauty which lies all about them.

Two other delegates, Messrs. A. G. Hannah and John Moffatt, insisted upon the importance of allowing children to draw in colour, as a help to the development of the imaginative faculties, quoting Mr. George Clausen, R.A., who said in one of his Academy lectures:

> A picture that is well drawn and modelled only will interest, but will be passed by in favour of colour. For colour touches us more deeply; its sense is more instructive. *A child will be excited by colours but indifferent to form.*

Certainly the colour sense is one of those finer faculties which should not be neglected by the educationist. Colour education is a refining influence which will help much in making the children's after-life beautiful, and the delegates were right in insisting on its importance.

How can we make too much of it, when we think of the thousands of children who step from our elementary schools into life, unaffected by the refining influence of colour education—to become workers without ideas of beauty—to furnish homes for themselves, and to be engaged, perhaps, in the manufacture of articles in which colour plays an important part—to possess as citizens, picture galleries containing priceless treasures which they are unable to enjoy? The culture necessary for the enjoyment of colour should not be possessed by the few. It is the birthright of everyone, and it should be on the conscience of those responsible for education to see that every child is afforded opportunities for acquiring it.

The traditions of Indian art bring into Indian national life a glorious colour-music, one of those subtle, refining influences which have moulded Indian character and elevated national culture. One of the bad effects of modern education in India has been the vulgarisation of Indian life by the killing of the colour sense. If that sense were not killed by our educational system there would be much less demand for aniline dyes than there is now, and much less deterioration of those handicrafts for which a refined colour sense is necessary. Indian educationists should always remember that the living traditions of Indian art afford them a valuable help in art teaching which teachers in Europe and America are deprived of. In the West, national art tradition is almost extinct, so that the teachers have only nature study and archæological study upon which to build up a national system of art teaching. There is therefore much confusion of ideas, owing to the conflict of different authorities, different methods of teaching and different interpretations of nature. This confusion gets still more confounded when the European teacher comes to teach in India. School teachers and students in India need not be left to study nature without any other artistic guide than their own imagination, as they have a sound national tradition to guide and inform them in their study of nature. In Indian schools students should study nature in the light given them by Indian art. Drawing as taught by

Indian Schools of art has been, not Indian art, but European, so that what art students have learnt has been art in a European and not an Indian sense. A student or teacher who does not fully understand and appreciate Indian art and culture can do no good to India by his European studies; so the practice of sending Indian students to Europe for art education, when they are totally ignorant of Indian art, is a most pernicious one which all Indians with real artistic understanding will discourage. The contempt which the English-educated Indian generally shows for Indian art is only the measure of his ignorance.

A very excellent method of training for young children, which can be used in conjunction with drawing as a means of developing the creative and imaginative faculties, is now being practised in a few of the more progressive of English schools, and has been highly recommended by some of the best educationists. It is based upon the experience acquired by Mrs. M. E. Boole from the study of child psychology, and has both a scientific and artistic aim. This reconciliation of purposes, which are often regarded as at variance with each other, is to my mind one of its greatest recommendations, for all true art is scientific, just as all true science is artistic. Both belong to the great rhythm of things which controls the working of what we call Nature, and it is only the ignorance or charlatanism of professors of science and art which makes them so often play at cross purposes in education.

Mrs. Boole is the widow of George Boole, the famous mathematician, who was said by Herbert Spencer to have made the greatest advance in logic since Aristotle. Since her husband's death she has devoted herself to educational work and to the explanation of the psychological bearing of Boole's mathematical investigations, which seems to have been only vaguely understood in Europe. It will probably be better appreciated in India. An extremely interesting letter written by her to Professor J. C. Bose on this subject is published in *The Ceylon National Review* for June 1909, in which Mrs. Boole endeavours to show how much western science in the nineteenth century is indebted to Indian thought. Most European scientists seem to be just as unconscious of this as European artists generally are of the immense influence which Indian thought exercised upon one of the greatest epochs of European art, which we call Gothic, as I have pointed out in my book on *Indian Sculpture and Painting*. When the science of psychology has outgrown its infancy in the West we shall understand these things better, and probably deal with educational questions in India more sanely than we do now. I would commend Mrs. Boole's letter to the careful study of all my readers.

The method of child training to which I referred, called 'A Rhythmic approach to Mathematics,' is explained in a little book (George Philip, 2s. 6d.)

written by Mrs. Somervell, one of Mrs. Boole's pupils. Its object, as explained in the introduction, is:

To train in young children certain perceptions *without the use of any intellectual statements whatever.* These perceptions, if awakened, without intellectual effort or explanation, will enable the child: (1) when the actual teaching of mathematics begins, to approach the subject, not as something new, strange and abstract, but as orderly explanations of experiences long familiar to him, and charged with pleasurable association; (2) to become aware that there are laws of intimate relations between number, form, movement and the process of thought; (3) by means of this sense of relation, to grow able to translate readily any of these into terms of any other.

There are also important indirect results—beautiful curves are produced by a process so simple and automatic that the most inartistic child can succeed in generating beauty by mere conscientious accuracy and the habit of doing this tends to produce a keen feeling for line. It has been noticed in some cases, where clean and pure colour has been used, that a remarkable sensitiveness to colour relation has grown. The habit which the work has been found to form, even in children of five and six years old, of constantly inventing patterns suggested by geometric form, which frequently grow into familiar natural forms, has the effect of keeping them harmlessly happy and busy in a way which satisfies the creative instinct; the bearing of this on the future health of the child can hardly be exaggerated.

The materials used are needle and threads of different colours and a series of cards on which a few simple geometric forms are printed to initiate the child into the method of work which is called curve-sewing. After a little practice on the given exercises the child is able to evolve beautiful forms in infinite variety by applying the same method to any other geometric basis, which the child can choose for itself. Without imposing any strain upon their nervous systems, this is, Mrs. Boole says in her Preface:

> A means of introducing little children to the conception of a connection between organic thought-sequence and the evolution of harmonious form . . . I gave two or three Christmas cards worked with curves to Mr. Garstang, Mathematical Master at Bedales School, Petersfield, who showed them to Miss Borsche, a Froebel teacher under Mr. Scott, Head Master of a Preparatory School, connected with Bedales, suggesting that she might try to invent some method of combining curves. She and her little class devoted only fifty minutes per week during school hours to sewing curves on cards, but some of the children practised of their own accord at spare moments, and soon began making combinations and suggestions of their own. The experiment was carefully watched to see whether the children were growing excited, fatigued, or unduly conscious of personal inspiration. But as no symptoms of any such danger showed themselves, the two Head Masters (of Bedales and the Preparatory School) showed their wisdom by giving Miss Borsche a free hand. Some of the work produced was shown by Mr. Garstang in January, 1904, at the house of Dr. Arthur Somervell; and the connection between harmonograph curves and those produced by Miss Borsche's pupils was pointed out. Mrs. Somervell then began experimenting, with very interesting results. This summer, I have had the great joy of seeing Mrs. Somervell and her children give lessons in

the art of geometric design to a few children attending the Primary School at Overstrand; and I have no hesitation in saying that the method carried out by Miss Borsche and Mrs. Somervell, with which they kindly wish to connect my name, is a working possibility as a means of truly national evocation of creative and organising power.

Mrs. Boole's method has, as she says, one great advantage over many kinds of educational reform : it can be put into operation without agitation or public discussion, without Acts of Parliament, or the permission of School Inspectors. This should make it particularly useful in India. Any intelligent father or mother can set the children to work at it. A complete outfit of the simple materials required for a family or small class together with three sets of the cards printed with geometric patterns, is supplied by the publishers of the book at the cost of five shillings, but country materials could be substituted at a much less expense. Those who wish to know more of Mrs. Boole's methods should read her books: *Preparation of the Child for Science, Logic taught by Love,* (C. W. Daniel) and *The Mathematical Psychology of Gratry and Boole* (G. P. Putnam).

CHAPTER IX

THE INDUSTRIAL PROBLEM AND THE HOME

I CANNOT too often repeat that the industrial regeneration of India is first and last a moral and intellectual problem, not a technical one. It must begin and end, not with processes and machinery, but in the mind of every Indian man or woman. According to your intellectual and moral ideal, so will India's future be shaped artistically, industrially and politically, "those who worship the ḍevas go to the ḍevas; those who worship the Piṭṛs, go to the Piṭṛs; those who worship the Bhuṭs, go to the Bhuṭs." If you strive to emulate the commercial ideal of modern Europe, India will cease to be India; it will inevitably become, as Mr. Cecil Burns described it—a "suburb of London and Paris". And this is certainly the ideal which a great many preachers of the Swaḍeshi doctrine make their own and hold up for the admiration of Indians.

Only a few weeks ago I noticed that the *Bengalee* of Calcutta, referring to the success of some so-called Swaḍeshi cotton mills recently established in Bengal, congratulated its readers that Serampore "bids fair to become the Manchester of Bengal". Now I would ask any Indian who has at heart the welfare of his fellow-countrymen to read the description of the condition of the Manchester industrial population given on a previous page, and then consider whether the methods of industrialism which have produced such frightful degeneration and depravity in Europe are worthy of imitation by Indian reformers.

Serampore, the one district in all India, in which swaḍeshi industrial methods have so far proved eminently successful, is that which has been chosen by Bengali 'patriots' for establishing *viḍeshi* power-loom factories which are now competing with the local handicraftsmen and diverting their profits into the pockets of the patriotic shareholders! In the Serampore district there are about 10,000 Bengali hand-weavers who have set an example of self-help to the rest of India by adapting European labour-saving appliances to their traditional craft practice. By this they have raised themselves to a condition of comparative prosperity, without any depreciation of the good Indian quality of their handiwork. By calling public attention to the example of these intelligent weavers, I started the movement for the revival of hand-loom weaving which has made such great strides in recent years in many different parts of India.

It would be natural to suppose that the organisers of the Swaḍeshi movement in Bengal would have been eager to help the remaining 400,000 weavers in the province to adopt the same labour-saving appliances and thus create an efficient indigenous industrial organisation. But this they have left to the unaided efforts of Government. Before I left India I succeeded in persuading the Government of Bengal to establish at Serampore a Central Weaving College, with affiliated schools in the other weaving centres of the province for the purpose of showing the hand-weavers of Bengal how they, with more perfect appliances, could hold their own against power-looms. Now, owing to the establishment of these 'Swaḍeshi' cotton mills at Serampore, the College, only opened six months ago, is already in danger of being diverted from its real purpose of aiding the indigenous hand-loom industry, owing to the clamour of a section of the students not belonging to the weaving caste to be taught European power-loom processes, with a view to getting employment in these 'Swaḍeshi' mills. It is hardly necessary to point out the injustice of using public funds for technical education, which mill-owners are quite able to provide for unaided, only to assist capitalists and middlemen in their efforts to destroy the village hand-loom industry which is in urgent need of better technical equipment. The injustice is none the less because the capitalists in this case happen to be Indians trading as Swaḍeshi reformers.

I can only hope that the Principal of the College will make a firm stand against this school-boy clamour. I had to face just the same kind of clamour in the Calcutta School of Art, when, some years ago, I persuaded the Government to dispose of a collection of European pictures and to use the proceeds for buying good examples of Indian sculpture and painting. The Indian Art Gallery established in Calcutta by this reform has been the starting point of the only really national Indian artistic movement of modern times—that of which Mr. Abanindro Nath Tagore and his pupils are the leaders. It is significant that the unreasoning clamour of the students and parents who opposed me then received strong support in the *Bengalee's* Editorial columns, where I was violently attacked because, it was said, I was ignorantly lowering the educational standard in art by adopting these Swaḍeshi principles. The same journal, by its support of the Indian capitalists who are exploiting the Swaḍeshi movement in Bengal, is now using its influence to frustrate the somewhat belated efforts of Government to assist Indian handicraftsmen in their struggle against the western competitive system, which is at the root of all the greatest social evils which afflict modern Europe. If the Serampore Weaving College is diverted from its original purpose and becomes only an instrument in the hands of self-seeking capitalists, it will be largely due to the misguided efforts of those Swaḍeshi politicians, whose western education makes them incapable of approaching Indian artistic and industrial problems from an Indian point of view.

The same incoherency of thought is shown in the present agitation for the repeal of the Excise duty on Indian power-loom fabrics, which has been receiving strong support from the Indian press. None of the Indian politicians who are demanding protection for indigenous industries seems to have realised that, from the Indian standpoint, this duty is wholly justifiable, because it gives a slight measure of protection to the indigenous hand-loom industry. Personally I think protection is an artificial and insufficient remedy, which organisation and education ought to render unnecessary. But if protection, as a temporary expedient, is right, then surely the first persons entitled to it are the millions of long-suffering, struggling, village weavers, and not the few hundreds of well-to-do shareholders of Indian power-loom mills whose pockets have been already well lined at the expense of the indigenous industry. Even assuming that the Excise duty has only been imposed in the interests of Lancashire capitalists, the fact that it assists the indigenous industry, until such time as proper organisation and educational methods shall make it able to help itself should commend it to the strong support of Indians who desire the greatest good for the greatest number of their fellow-countrymen.

The Swaḍeshi movement will be utterly discredited in the eyes of all right-minded Indians if, instead of holding up a truly Indian ideal of life and work it is used to exploit Indian Industry only for the selfish interests of capitalists and middlemen, as industry has been exploited by capitalists and middlemen in modern Europe. The Indian industrial ideal must not be that of Manchester and Birmingham.

When a new Indian ideal of life has grown out of the national consciousness fully informed by the wisdom of both East and West and guided by the experience of both good and evil—knowing the good to be good and the evil to be evil—that ideal will be the motive power which will restore the industrial vitality of India. The solution of the artistic problem is the solution of the industrial problem also; the key to both is to be found in learning to live well. And as life is begun first in the home, and not in the school or work-shop, so it is in the home that the foundation of India's industrial regeneration must be laid, whether that home be a hut or a palace.

It is not given to every Indian to arrive at that full knowledge which will enable him to create an ideal Indian home; but it is certainly open to every Swaḍeshi politician to practise in his home the principles which he preaches in public. Without this practice it will be impossible for him to gain the power of discrimination which will make his judgment sound in artistic and industrial questions, and, without that power of discrimination added to it, the Swaḍeshi movement will never revitalise Indian art and industry.

There is a lamentable want of discrimination in the Indian who excludes everything Indian from his home because he believes that everything European is superior and that his preference for European pictures, Brussels carpets and Tottenham Court Road furniture proves his superior educated taste. But Indian reformers who preach the Swaḍeshi doctrine must be careful that they do not fall into the opposite error, and assume that all things are good because they are called Swaḍeshi. A great many things called Indian are neither good as art nor are they really Indian. Especially is this the case with that class of things, known to Europeans as Indian 'art ware,' which fill the shops of Indian curiosity dealers, and represent Indian art in Exhibitions in Europe. The reason for their badness as art is sufficiently indicated by the name applied to them: they do not belong to real life and work, they are 'curiosities'—freaks of art produced for the amusement of those who stand entirely aloof from true Indian culture.

Look for the motive or idea by which every work of art is produced, for in it you will discover the measure of its merit or demerit. Those whose Swaḍeshi sentiments are mainly governed by the idea of political or commercial advantage will not understand or produce good Swaḍeshi art, or create true Swaḍeshi homes. It is not enough to banish from the Indian home crude Brussels carpets, Brummagem chandeliers, tenth-rate European pictures, sculpture, and furniture, only to replace them by equally bad Indian carpets, furniture, sculpture, and pictures. The same want of discrimination which has made even the best educated Indians, and those to whom expense is no consideration, place their artistic consciences in the keeping of European shop-keepers and picture-dealers, will make them equally indiscriminative in choosing Indian things. It is not easy for Indians without artistic education to discriminate, even in Indian art, because for the last fifty years India has been ransacked for all its portable art treasures — the things which were formerly part of the domestic life of cultured Indians—to fill European Art Museums and private collections; so that, except in ancient monuments and in a very few Museums in India, there is little left which is representative of the highest standard of Indian domestic art. Indians have despised their own art and have willingly exchanged their best art productions for European things of a vastly lower artistic standard. In China and Japan, in spite of the invasion of European fashions, the best works of indigenous art have been so highly valued that very few European Museums or private collectors have been willing to pay the local market value for them, so comparatively few of the best things have found their way to Europe.

But such books as Dr. Coomāraswāmy's on Sinhalese domestic art could easily be supplemented by others, were there a demand for them, and India still has an industrial asset of higher value than even the most precious works of antiquity in the living tradition of her craftsmen. Given the intellectual and moral impulse, it is much easier to restore the artistic standard in Indian domestic life than it is in Europe, where the old craft traditions have been almost obliterated by the industrial methods of the last two centuries and by the insatiate greed of the capitalist.

There is a curious want of discrimination, which is shown even by those Indians of the wealthy and aristocratic classes who in their intimate domestic life still keep up more or less Indian artistic traditions, in the almost universal custom of furnishing in a *quasi*-European fashion the part of their house or palace in which they receive their European guests. It is done out of a mistaken sense of hospitality and courtesy, but the real effect of the custom is to emphasise and strengthen the social barrier which exists between the Anglo-Indian and Indian communities. Nothing would tend to draw the two communities closer together more than the feeling that there was somewhere a meeting ground in social life, where East could be West, and West, East. But this custom simply proclaims to the world at large that there cannot be an approach from both sides, that East can go to the West but never can West go

East. To all Europeans who earnestly desire to gain a closer aquaintance with real Indian life and thought it is a disappointment to find themselves in the atmosphere of suburban England when they are invited to enter an Indian household. It cannot be flattering to an intelligent European to be presented with what is hardly ever better than a travesty of Western artistic culture, and for those who believe that future social progress in the world lies in a blending of eastern and western ideals it is grievous to discover that even in the opportunities for social intercourse which Indians themselves provide for us, unnecessary obstacles are put in the way of a true appreciation of the Indian social ideal.

It is very true, that, among uninformed Europeans, there is a general assumption that India is a savage country which it is England's divine mission to civilise. But when English-educated Indians themselves often present to their European guests no higher domestic ideal than that of a London boarding house, and speak of their fellow-countrymen who keep to the Indian tradition of domestic life as 'jungly' folk, it is not surprising that the same belief should be prevalent among Anglo-Indians also. No doubt many Anglo-Indians are as much in need of art education as Indians, but I believe that if some of the leaders of Indian Society were to set the example of having their reception rooms decorated in a good Indian style, with good Indian pictures and sculpture and furniture designed after good Indian models, the change would be welcomed by all the most cultured of Anglo-Indian Society and it would tend to put the social relations between Indians and Europeans upon a much better footing, for nothing tends to promote misunderstanding more than social customs which imply a feeling of social inequality.

Besides bringing a more wholesome atmosphere into social relations, the change would certainly have a very good effect upon Indian industrial conditions. It would give more opportunities for Indian craftsmen and for students of Indian Schools of Art; and Anglo-Indian firms which now only teach Indian craftsmen to imitate European designs would quickly find it to their advantage to allow their designers to work on Indian traditional lines. The home is the microcosm of the State. The first endeavour of industrial reformers should be to establish a healthy psychological atmosphere in the home, for the psychology of home-life largely determines the industrial conditions of the nation.

As the home is *par excellence* woman's sphere, the true ideal of the Swaḍeshi home will be found in the minds of women, rather than of men. Very few of the English-educated Indian men of this generation possess the discrimination to distinguish between good art and bad, and but for the intuitive sense and spirituality of Indian women Indian art would have sunk much lower than it has done. It is their influence in the home, and not any political or commercial propaganda, which has given the Swadeshi movement whatever real vitality it possesses; and it will be by their work in the home, rather than by the craftsman's intelligence, that India will be saved from falling into the quagmire of western commercialism, if saved it will be. Indian women will not reckon India's progress by counting the factory chimneys.

Hitherto the psychological aspect of the industrial problem seems to have been totally disregarded by most Swadeshi reformers. They have looked everywhere abroad for its solution—to Europe, America and Japan—they cry out for foreign machinery, for foreign technical experts, technical schools, schools of art, industrial conferences, etc., etc., (all on foreign models) to help India out of its difficulty. They rail at Indian art and at the great caste organisation of Indian industry which once made India the greatest industrial country of the world; they pray for more political enfranchisement, so that they may hasten the day when India has her Manchester and Birmingham, without knowing what they pray for. All this outcry only tends to the unmaking of India and to the destruction of all Indian ideals; it is the industrial application of Macaulay's foolish dictum that all India's literary culture was not worth a single bookshelf of a good European library. It is a blind leading of the blind.

Indian industry has declined less from the competition of European science and machinery, than from the psychological degeneracy of the Indian home. There is profound truth in what Dr. Coomāraswāmy, with his knowledge of all that western industrialism has achieved, tells you:

> If we loved and understood Indian art we should know that even now the Indian craftsman could, if we would let him, build for us and clothe us in ways of beauty that could not be attained in modern Europe for any expenditure of money at all. We could, if we would, even to-day, live like the very gods; but we lust after the fleshpots of Egypt, and deservedly our economy suffers.

This psychological degeneracy began in times long anterior to British rule; had it not been so there would have been no British rule. British rule gives you the opportunity to make a new India stronger and greater than it has ever been, if you will but begin the regeneration of India's industrialism, where the mainsprings of all industry necessary for a good and healthy life are centred—in the home.

When the ancient lawgivers of India laid down regulations for the four great castes their intention was not to create impassable racial and social barriers, but to unite all the members of the great Hinḍū family together on a basis of mutual co-operation. Each member of the caste family had his or her special duties to perform, but these were not to make them consider themselves independent of each other, or to forget the unity of the whole family. The father was the intellectual and spiritual head of the family. The sons were the protectors of the household in war and breadwinners in peace; they were also the master-builders skilled in the higher crafts. To the mother and daughters fell the most important household duties, which included the finer artistic work—the adornment of the home and the weaving of apparel; to the servants the rough and menial work.

So long as each member of the family not only fulfilled the duties of his or her particular sphere, but was mindful of mutual obligations, so long as the father helped the sons, the sons the mother and daughters—so long, in fact, as the fourfold division of caste duties was on a real, co-operative basis—India remained great and strong. But when the idea of pollution crept in; when the head of the family, forgetting his obligations to the other members, shut himself up in a corner of the house and refused access to the rest of the household, lest his spiritual vocation should be lowered in dignity by contact with worldly affairs; when each member was concerned only with the duties of his or her caste, then caste became a source of weakness instead of strength, the family lost its cohesion and India became an easy prey to every foreign invader. Caste is not necessarily an evil; so long as the unity of the family is not forgotten, it is a splendid institution for concentrating the national strength and making the best use of it. Caste has been the salvation of Indian art and industry during the critical period of transition through which India is now passing, and the caste traditions are still the most valuable industrial asset India possesses.

What India wants is not the entire abolition of caste traditions, but the restoration of the artistic and industrial cohesion of the whole caste family. English education, so far as it has helped to restore the political cohesion of India has been a great national gain; but this advantage seems to have blinded English-educated Indians to the fact that owing to its one-sided character their education has been, artistically and industrially, the disintegrating factor which has brought confusion and discord into the Indian household. If Swaḍeshi politicians are wise they will let harmony be restored by ceasing to invite outsiders into their own domestic concerns, and leave to the Indian housewife the task of setting her house in order again.

As an outsider myself, I am loath to intrude my advice upon the Indian housewife, but a Madrasi gentleman, Mr. M. C. Nañjunda Row, M. B., F. C. S., lately sent me a paper written by him for the Mysore Dassera Industrial and Agricultural Exhibition of 1911, which contains many excellent suggestions for her. He says:

There is waiting to be utilised an enormous quantity of hand-power in our homes, and the special purpose of this paper is to lay stress on the importance of home, or domestic industries, as distinguished from cottage industries . . . In India, until a few centuries ago, the daughters of Eve span even when the sons of Adam remained idle and abstained from digging. The humming sound of the spinning wheel of the Punjabi peasant women is said to have kept time and tune with the repetition of the *Hamsa mantram* (*Sivoham Sivoham Sivoham*) by them.

The rigid observance of the caste distinctions by the Brāhmaṇas who, he says, assigned manual labour to the Suḍra caste, helped to disturb the old routine of family life: it resulted in the dethronement of the dignity of labour, and made idle gossips of the ladies.

It is not quite accurate to say that manual labour was originally assigned to the Suḍra caste. Even at the present day some of the higher Hindū craftsmen claim equality with Brāhmaṇas. In the *Rāmāyaṇa* the priests themselves carved the sacrificial posts, and the craftsmen who assisted at sacrifices were accorded equal honour with the priests. But it is certainly true that, owing to various causes, the old ideal of the Indian household has degenerated, to the great detriment of the economic status of the whole Indian community. I believe there still survives in Assam, and probably in other parts of India, an old tradition of the Indian household, that the unmarried daughters even in the highest social position, should spin and weave the garments required for their own wedding outfit and for that of their future husbands. The practice of such handicrafts was an essential part of domestic life in mediæval Europe, from the royal palace down to the peasant's cottage, and from the creative energy thus generated in every household was produced the great industrial developments of modern Europe. If all Indian ladies, especially those of the higher and middle classes, were to re-introduce this admirable custom into their households it would go a long way towards solving the industrial problem of India.

Mr. Nañjunda Row seems to be mostly concerned in providing an additional means of livelihood for indigent middle class families and from this standpoint his suggestions are well worth consideration. But I should regard the psychological aspect of the question as of much greater importance. When the psychological atmosphere of the Indian household, from the highest to the lowest, is re-charged with creative energy, then the immense powers of the traditional Indian industrial system will no longer be wasted in such a blind and foolish fashion as they are now. The Indian caste family will be replaced on its old co-operative footing and with the revived power of artistic discrimination India will choose wisely her own ways of industrial reformation, which will be better than any which foreign experts can prescribe for her.

CHAPTER X

THE ETHICS OF MACHINERY

When the cultured Indian woman begins, as I suggested in my last chapter, to resume her traditional artistic vocation in the household, not for any pecuniary profit, but for love of India, and with enthusiasm for her high spiritual mission, she will find ready at hand practically all the material she needs to work with, without any foreign importations. For the adornment of the Indian home the Indian artists and craftsmen she would wish to employ need no technical education and no examples other than the great achievements of their ancestors; their tools and processes differ little from those of artists and first class craftsmen in modern Europe. The implements of Indian arts and crafts have by many centuries of practice been brought to a high pitch of perfection for purely artistic purposes, and Europe has very little to teach India in this respect. In fact, when artistic quality only is sought for, Europe even now is not above learning technique from the oriental craftsman. The best carpets and brocades in Europe are still made on the same loom and by the same method as the Indian weaver uses, but not even the best skill of Europe has ever rivalled the masterpieces which the cunning fingers of the Oriental has woven, and could again weave were the opportunity given. Similarly the best cotton prints in Europe are printed by hand-blocks, just as they have always been printed by the Indian cotton printer. The most artistic bronzes are cast by the same process as the Indian metal-worker uses.

Not even the wealthiest in Europe can command such abundant service of skilled craftsmen as the well-to-do Indian housewife can command, if she will. It is the psychological impulse, not education or mechanical improvements, that is needed for the revival of Indian craft in the Indian home. When the psychological impulse comes the verandahs and courtyards of Indian palaces and mansions will again be thronged with busy Indian craftsmen, as they were in the palmy days of Indian art; the broken threads which bound the artistic castes to the other members of the Hiṇdū family will be mended, and the web of Indian life, losing the drab dullness of modern materialism, will shine again with all the beauty of colour and broidery which higher spiritual and intellectual ideals will work into it.

But the mission of Indian womanhood covers a yet wider sphere: it extends to every Indian household, and is not confined to the palaces and mansions of the high-born and wealthy. With their own fingers, Indian women of high and low degree must spin and weave to revive the artistic power of the Indian race, to make that power part of their own and their children's physical and mental being, and thus recharge the whole psychological atmosphere of their homes with creative energy.

In this noble task which must begin with the re-birth of Indian art and craftsmanship, the mechanical inventions of modern Europe will be more often a hindrance than a help. Art is created by the human mind and body, not by a machine. Mechanical apparatus in art and the higher crafts is only an artificial means of applying the psychical and physical power of the human being: it can never add to it or be a substitute for it. The household loom used by many European ladies in the present day is not one of the latest mechanical inventions, but the common loom of two hundred years ago, and on such ordinary looms many ladies in Europe now weave their own dress material, as was the custom in the middle ages, and even carpets for their own drawing-rooms. The technical traditions of the Indian weaver supply all that India requires for this purpose, though in the preparation of the thread for the loom some of the tedium of old Indian methods may be lessened by European appliances. It is of vital importance for Swaḍeshi reformers to understand the ethics of machinery and their application to India's industrial problem. This is a point on which there is a great deal of wrong thinking and wrong doing, even on the part of many self-constituted art experts, especially those who regard art as only a by-study in modern experimental science. Art is a science—the greatest of all sciences—but its theoretical principles, unlike many of those of modern experimental science, are fundamental and unchangeable. Art aims at perfection, and so does science, properly applied. But modern commercialism has not properly applied modern scientific and mechanical inventions. It has used them not for perfecting the products of human industry or for promoting the social and intellectual advancement of the human race, but as instruments for bringing down quality to the lowest possible level which will both satisfy uneducated tastes and add to the profits of the manufacturer.

A very large part of the most ingenious machinery used in modern manufacture is not for the purpose of making a thing better than it was made before, but for the purpose of making it appear better than it is. According to the ethics of art a dye is applied to textile fabrics to add the charm of beautiful colour to the beauty of good material. But according to the ethics of modern manufacturing science it is added to conceal the badness of the material. Similarly in good weaving, according to artistic principles a fabric is finished when it leaves the loom; but in modern textile manufacture a new department of industry has been created, called 'finishing,' in which the most ingenious machinery is used to give a superficial appearance of finish to material which when it leaves the loom is unsaleable—the 'finish' conceals the inferiority of the fabric.

Good handicraft educates public taste and morals: modern manufacturing processes debase them. The handicraftsman works for an educated public which prefers one good thing to two inferior. Machinery in art manufacture supplies the demand of a public which ignorantly exchanges old lamps for new, only craving for novelty and not knowing what is good and what is bad. A great deal of what is called progress in European industry is only a return to old principles which are still practised by the best Indian craftsmen; for instance, in the masterpieces of ancient weaving, pottery, stained glass, etc., which are stored in European art museums for the education of the public, much of the beauty of colour is owing to irregularities produced in the process of hand manufacture. A good oriental carpet is beautiful because each colour is not uniform throughout, as in a machine-made carpet, but varied in different parts, the variation being produced by the absence of uniformity in the dyeing of the wool. The latter is dyed in small quantities at a time, each dyeing producing some slight variation in colour. Similarly in ancient stained glass manufacture the colouring-matter was, by the hand process, not evenly distributed throughout the material, and the irregularities thus produced in the sheets of glass gave the wonderful jewel-like quality to the windows of mediæval Gothic Cathedrals.

Modern European commercialism, only intent on cheapness, eliminated these irregularities, which from an artistic point of view are priceless, in order to reduce the cost of manufacture: for an ordinary machine cannot reproduce irregularities—absolute uniformity is the normal product of a good machine. It does not pay a modern manufacturer, working for an uneducated public, to prepare the dyes in small quantities for each carpet he makes. He must manufacture things by hundreds and thousands, all exactly uniform in colour and material. The uneducated masses, both in Europe and India, prefer a carpet which is perfectly even and monotonous in colour: they dislike any thing uneven or irregular, and the greater beauty of good hand-work does not appeal to them. But since a regular system of national art training has been established by European Governments, through hundreds of art and technical schools connected with art museums in which the great works of ancient and mediæval handicraft are stored, manufacturers have now to provide for a considerable section of the public whose taste is better educated. These people demand more artistic work and since they are prepared to pay for it, many of the best European manufacturers have returned partially or wholly to the old hand processes which are practically the same as those of the best

Indian craftsmen of the present day. Even the machine manufacturers now begin to imitate hand productions by using machines in which the irregularities of hand manufacture are ingeniously imitated. These imitations no more deceive an educated eye than a gramophone or pianola deceive an educated ear, but many people, only half-educated in art, are satisfied with these imitations just as they are satisfied with gramophones and pianolas.

There exist in Europe at the present day three grades of art maufacturers :—

I. The highest grade, which has returned, wholly or partially, to the principles of oriental art industry, formerly practised in Europe.

II. The mechanical manufacturer who imitates the productions of the first grade by means of machinery.

III. The mechanical manufacturer who works for the least educated masses, whose ideals are only novelty and cheapness.

The essential method of these two lower grades may be described in Dr. Coomâraswâmy's words. It is :

> To create a want in order to have the opportunity of profiting by the filling of it. Under the commercial system, it is no longer demand that regulates supply, but production that 'forces a market'. Machinery has enabled the capitalist to do this to the fullest extent. The promise of labour-saving machinery was a millennium for the worker, shorter hours and easier

work ; its results have been merely increased production, increased profit to the capitalist, and not less work, but less intelligent work for the producer. Not merely is the workman, through division of labour, no longer able to make any whole thing; not only is he confined to making small parts of things ; but it is impossible for him to improve his position, or to win reward for excellence in the craft itself. Under guild conditions, it was possible and usual for the apprentice to rise through all the grades of knowledge and experience to the position of a master-craftsman. But take any such trade as carpet-making under modern conditions by power-looms. The operator has no longer to design or to weave in and out the threads with his own fingers. He is employed in reality, not as a carpet weaver, but as the tender of a machine. He may rise to a higher place it is true—but it is to the place of a man responsible for the successful running of many machines by many men. That craft is for him destroyed as a means of culture, and the community has lost one more man's intelligence—for it is obviously futile to attempt to build up by evening classes and free libraries what the whole of a man's work is for ever breaking down. It is no longer possible for culture and refinement to come to the craftsman through his work : he must seek them in the brief hours snatched from rest and sleep, at the expense of life itself. It is not strange that he does not seek them, nor that the expression is lacking in his work. He has not even the capacity for idling, but must continually seek amusement and excitement. There can be no quality of leisure in his work. In short, commercial production absolutely forbids a union of art with labour. It is instructive to compare the still living, but fast disappearing relics of this union in the East with the results of western endeavours through education and free libraries, to restore that general culture which cannot under commercialism exist; not there does the ploughman speak as elegantly as the courtier, not there are riches little valued; nor can these things be where life is lived, not as an art, but as a wild beast fight.

But in Europe, as civilisation and artistic culture slowly but surely become deeper and more widely diffused among the masses, the tendency is towards an increase in the highest grades of art manufacturers and a diminution in the lower grades. No one can dispute that this is a healthy and right tendency. In India, there is just the opposite tendency, which is encouraged both officially and by Swaḍeshi reformers. In India the highest grade of art manufacture, which is represented by the millions of handicraftsmen belonging to the traditional artistic castes, is comparatively much more common than it is in Europe. As the skill of the trained handicraftsman is of a much higher order than the skill of the factory hand who only looks after the working of a machine, India can command in almost every important branch of art manufacture a much higher average of technical skill than is to be found in any branch of European art manufacture. The difficulty of the situation in India is that the handicraftsman is artistically much better educated than the so-called 'educated' classes to which he must look for employment. The Indian handicraftsman represents an older and higher state of national artistic culture, which is rapidly being degraded by the denationalising process now called education. Surely, the right policy in India, then, is to bring education up to the same level as that of the handicraftsman; to throw wide open the doors of the University to art, and to use all the influence of the State to encourage the highest class of art manufacture, and to improve the social condition of the art workman.

The official policy, and that of most Swaḍeshi reformers, has been just the reverse of this and diametrically opposed to what is now recognised to be sound artistic policy in Europe. Art administration in India is and has been for the last fifty years, little better than waste of public money. The art interests of India represent a far larger economic value than that of the whole of the present educational system, yet these interests are supposed to be sufficiently safeguarded by one school in a province larger than Great Britain, which has its hundreds of art schools and thousands of art classes. The head of this one school is often not a trained art expert; but if that were otherwise his authority is so small that in the last twenty-five years, as I can testify from personal experience, the only experts whose advice has been listened to departmentally, are scientists who through artistic ignorance, or half-knowledge, bring all the influence of the State to make the Indian handicraftsman the tool of self-seeking capitalists, and to drag down the standard of art manufacture to the level of second- and third-rate European manufacturers.

Most Indian Swadeshi reformers are foolish enough to follow this lead, not seeing that by so doing they are only playing the game of European commercialism and hastening the denationalisation which is the degradation of Indian art and industry.

Lord Curzon was voicing the opinions of his departmental scientific advisers when he declared at the Delhi Durbar that it was inevitable that the hand-loom should be superseded by the power-loom, just as the hand-puṅkāh was being superseded by the electric fan. This is a totally false analogy. No artistic operation will ever be entirely accomplished by mechanical means. Even plain weaving is to a great extent an artistic operation, and will remain so to the end of time. The extent to which weaving will continue to be an artistic operation depends locally upon the degree of artistic culture, or civilisation, reached by the community which uses the process. It cannot be the assumption of any civilised Government that India must inevitably be deprived of all artistic culture, and thus have no further need for the hand-loom.

The question which has to be answered is whether the Indian hand-weaver can supply the wants of the uneducated masses, or of those people who require good and cheap clothing, but have not reached a sufficiently high state of culture to appreciate artistic quality. If he cannot, then hand-weaving in India will be limited to meeting the demands of the richer and more cultivated classes. If he can, it will be so much the better for the poorer and less educated classes that they are clothed with more artistic material than the power-loom can supply, and very much better for the whole community that the skilled handicraftsman is not degraded into a factory workman minding a machine.

For answering this question, it is necessary to realise whether weaving is one of those operations in which steam or electric power has an inherent superiority over hand labour. There are many operations in which the superiority of the former is incontestable, such as the lifting or dragging of heavy weights, or working with masses of material too large, too heavy, or too intractable for a single man to deal with, also in work where extreme regularity, uniformity and mechanical precision are indispensable. When a huge mass of iron has to be welded into shape it is easy to understand that a steam hammer, in which the force of a hundred blacksmiths' arms are concentrated is a more effective tool than he human. Railway engines, steamships, steam or hydraulic cranes, and hundreds of similar things, unnecessary to particularise, are examples in which mechanical power has an inherent superiority over manual labour. But a loom is a machine in which the force required to work it does not usually exceed the strength of one man, and any excess of the force required absolutely prevents good weaving. In all countries where skilled manual labour is plentiful and cheap the power-loom has no inherent superiority over the hand-loom, provided that the lat er is made as mechanically perfect as the former, so that the working power of the hand-weaver is not wasted. The only question is, whether the unit of mechanical power can be produced at a cheaper rate than the average cost of manual power.

CHAPTER XI

THE DECENTRALISATION OF INDUSTRY IN EUROPE

FOR the lowest grades of weaving, that is, for textiles such as packing material, gunny cloth, etc., required for purely utilitarian purposes, it is probable that hand-labour will eventually be superseded entirely by purely mechanical processes, for the proper function of the mechanical power is to relieve mankind of the drudgery of labour. But India will not learn the proper functions of machinery by copying the methods of European commercialism as she is doing now. Mr. C. R. Ashbee, M.A., one of the leaders of the Arts and Crafts movement in England, says, in his introduction to Dr. Coomaraswamy's *Indian Craftsman* that, owing to the abuse of machinery in Europe, it is possible that the destruction and waste it brings equal the gain it yields.

Trained as we are to measure everything by a mechanical standard, it is difficult for us to see things clearly, to get a correct focus. We are apt to forget that our view is biased, that we attach a disproportionate value to the productions of machinery, and that a vast number, perhaps sixty per cent. of these productions are not, as is generally supposed, labour-saving, health-giving and serviceable to our general life and culture, but the reverse. 'It is questionable,' said John Stuart Mill half a century ago, 'whether all the labour-saving machinery has yet lightened the day's labour of a single human being;' and the years that have followed his death seem only to have further borne out his statement, but the people themselves who are being exploited by mechanical conditions are beginning to find it out.

Directly the smallest element of artistic beauty enters into textile manufacture, as it does in the weaving of the national *dhoṭi* or *sāri* of even the poorest Indian man or woman, then the hand process has always an incontestable and inherent superiority over the mechanical process. The higher the artistic quality required, the greater becomes the superiority of the hand-process. The power-loom will never entirely supersede the hand-loom as long as the desire for beauty is inherent in human nature; and to put forward the doctrine that the hand-loom will be inevitably superseded by the power-loom merely proves how utterly incapable most official experts are of understanding India's industrial problem.

Every hand-loom weaver who is driven into a power-loom factory is a lowering of India's industrial efficiency, and a depreciation of her artistic, intellectual and moral standard. For, though I have said that in the lowest grades of weaving it is probable that hand-labour will eventually be superseded by automatic machinery, it by no means follows that weaving, even in these lowest grades, will wholly cease to be a domestic or cottage industry. In India the official theory is that all Indian industry, like the official administration, must be centralised—which means that the millions of skilled hand-weavers (who are some of the most skilful artisans of the world) which India possesses, must all be concentrated in the great Anglo-Indian industrial cities, and delivered, body and soul, into the hands of Indian and European capitalists, the 'captains of industry' who play the modern commercial game with their fellow-creatures for pawns.

In industrial as in artistic policy, the present Indian administration is many years behind the times. The centralisation of industry began in Europe about a century ago with the introduction of the steam-engine. In the early days of steam power, the concentration of labour or the factory system was necessary in all branches of mechanical manufacture, because no means were known of distributing the power over long distances or over great areas. Anglo-Indian industrial experts seem to be utterly ignorant of the changed conditions brought about in Europe by electric power, which can be easily distributed over long distances and over great areas. The one man power required for a weaver's loom can now be distributed by electricity over an area of a square mile more easily than it can be distributed over a quarter of an acre by the steam-engine alone. Every year, improvements in electrical science make the distribution and subdivision of power easier and more economical, which means that every year the factory system becomes less indispensable than it was fifty years ago. Scientists now point to the utilisation of the heat of the sun as the future universal source of industrial power. Think what that means for Indian village industry!

In Europe the latest industrial development is not centralisation, but decentralisation. The mechanical power which fifty years ago could only be used economically in large factories, can now be used in the small workshop, and even brought to the workman's own home. The artisan is being emancipated from the tyranny of the factory. In Germany, the most scientific country of Europe, power-loom weaving is being already started as a cottage industry. The ideal loom of the future will be one in which either hand power or electric power can be used on different parts of the same fabric, the weaver changing from one to the other at his discretion, according to the character of the weaving. Then the workman will again become the master of the machine, instead of its slave.

It should be obvious to anyone who studies carefully the facts I have given, that it is either stupendous folly or wickedness to waste the inherited skill of the Indian village weaver by forcing him into power-loom factories as a means of educating him in the science of modern industry. It is usual to draw a distinction between the 'moral' and 'material' progress of India, though the progress which is not moral is not real progress. The moral factor dominates even the machine.

An interesting illustration of this is being shown in the streets of London at the present moment, one which is very pertinent to the question of Indian industrial development, especially to the revival of the great hand-loom industry. The hansom-cab and other horse-drawn vehicles are rapidly being superseded in the streets of London by motor vehicles. It might be supposed that here was a case in which the advantages of capitalism and of the centralisation of industry would become clearly evident. With a horse-drawn vehicle it is easy to understand that the personal interest of the driver and his kindness towards his horses are most important economic factors which give the small proprietor an advantage over the joint-stock company. But when the automatic machine takes the place of the living animal it might be imagined that these factors would be almost entirely eliminated, and that all the advantages would be on the side of the owners of large capital and great centralised organisations controlling a large number of motor vehicles. But so far from this being the case, it is the small proprietor, the owner of one or two of these motor vehicles who is gaining the advantage.

An interesting article in *The Morning Post* explains the reason for this. The moral factor rules even the motor cab. The writer says:

> The future of the taximeter cab proposition in the Metropolis, presents a very interesting problem. Doubtless the general impression is that only the very large cab companies will stand any chance of surviving. A first-hand investigation of the facts, however, leads one to precisely the opposite conclusion. The profitable running of a motor-cab can be achieved only by consciousness on the part of the driver and by a voluntary attention to a number of details such as cannot possibly be undertaken in any vast organisation where a cab is merely a cab and a driver is merely a man, without, as it were, individuality. For example, in a large cab company, if a man takes a holiday his vehicle is naturally not kept idle, but is taken out by another driver. Anybody who knows anything of machinery will realise at once that for a vehicle to be driven by two distinct drivers is ruination. Again, how is any big company to check the manner in which the drivers 'slap the cabs about,' jamming on the brakes and doing all sorts of dashing performances that they would certainly never indulge in if the machines were their own property. In many cases the whole difference in running a motor-cab at a loss or a profit lies in whether you tear your tyres by the abuse of the brakes resulting from reckless driving.

The writer goes on to show how the big companies, far from getting a choice of the best drivers, only get those that the small proprietors do not desire to employ. The small proprietors earn more themselves, and thus can afford to pay their employees better wages than the big companies give. Their employees in their turn, knowing the establishment is worked on a small scale, handle the machine with care in place of abusing it, because they know that if it goes out of work they go out of work also. These cabmen of the small proprietors are thrifty, sober men whose object it is to save money until they have sufficient to become small proprietors themselves.

Manufacturers state that there are no clients they trust more willingly than cabmen. . . . This development of the small proprietor and the honest cab-driver with enterprise, is one of considerable interest. They are likely to form a class that will increase considerably. The financial future for the large cab-companies is not bright, for the capital sunk in them is enormous, and, in the main, every extra machine that is put on the road tends, not so much to bring in additional receipts as to reduce the takings of the other cabs of the company on the road. One allows that in regard to repair works, motor-house facilities, and so forth, there are all the materials and there is all the special accommodation that can be desired. But these are not the only essentials for financial success, and the small man, in more or less of a make-shift stable, can for many reasons make far more profit per cab than the large companies.

The article further explains in detail how the big company system tends to make the motor cabmen not only careless and idle workers, but deliberately dishonest in their dealings with their employers. Like the power-loom factory system, this over-centralisation of work is economically unsound because it demoralises the workers. No progress is possible, either in art or in industry, when the moral factor is ignored. The Swaḍeshi movement will stand or fall, not by its success as a political manœuvre, nor by the increase it brings to the number of joint-stock trading companies and to the fatness of their dividends, but by its power to help in the moral uplifting of the Indian workman. So far as I have been able to observe, it has hitherto done more towards putting money into the pockets of middle class shareholders, by the usual processes of western commercialism, than towards the promotion of economic and moral efficiency on the part of the Indian handicraftsman. It is true that the demand for Swaḍeshi manufactures has kept the village weavers busy for a time and sent many unemployed back to their looms. This is good, so far as it goes and as long as it lasts. But unless Swaḍeshi reformers work hard to teach the village weavers to organise themselves and to improve their mechanical methods, how long will the Indian handicraftsman be able to stand against the 'Swaḍeshi' power-loom and large hand-loom factories which are being multiplied day by day to help the middle class Indian capitalist to make larger profits? One hears much in the Indian Press about Swaḍeshi factories and joint-stock companies, but very little of Indian handicraft, which is a greater moral factor than all of these.

India will cease to be India, but will not in the long run gain a single rupee, by ignoring the moral factor in her industrial organisation. The modern industrial system in Europe is in a great measure a temporary expedient based on the transitional character, or imperfection, of modern scientific developments. If India is to be spared in future generations, the great social conflict which now threatens Europe, her industrial reformers must look to the future, and not to the present, of European progress. India should lead and not follow.

CHAPTER XII

HAND-LOOM WEAVING

TAKING for granted the axiom that it is to India's best interest, morally, intellectually and economically, that the traditional organisation of her handicrafts should not be broken up and supplanted by the methods of modern commercialism but strengthened and developed in every possible way on its traditional foundation—the question arises, how can this strengthening and development be effected?

A better artistic understanding on the part of English-educated Indians, and better official administration, would tend automatically to revive the sumptuary handicrafts which are always developed by the higher æsthetic culture of civilised communities, for they have only degenerated by the lowering of æsthetic culture which has accompanied British administration and English education. But the lower grades of handicraft, which depend partly on the necessities and partly on the luxuries, of the poorest of the population, stand on a different footing. Of course, even a wealthy person will, in ordinary circumstances, but in the cheapest market provided that he gets the quality he desires; but sumptuary productions for the upper classes have not, even in Europe, been affected by modern mechanical science to anything like the same extent as articles of necessity, because, as I have tried to explain, the highest artistic quality can only be produced by the methods of the handicraftsman, and not by the methods of the mechanic. No improvement in mechanical science can alter this fundamental law. It is not the methods of the Indian sculptor, painter, or master-builder, nor those of the Benares kincob weaver, nor of the best Indian goldsmiths, which have kept behind the times. Their methods remain as good as the best of Europe are now. It is the Indian princes and other English-educated patrons of the native artist and handicraftsman who have fallen behind the times in artistic discrimination: when they become up-to-date in their European education Indian craftsmanship will need no outside help or Government aid.

But with the great majority of India's industrial population—the millions of handicraftsmen who provide the necessities of civilised life to the mass of the population—the case is different. The public they work for demands cheapness more than artistic quality, and it is imperative that, whenever possible, they should be equipped with efficient tools and apparatus to meet the competition of machine-made productions. It is impossible for me to go over the whole range of Indian handicraft and show what help can be given in each case, so I will confine myself to the question of hand-loom weaving, which is still the backbone of Indian industry and of much greater economic importance than any other, though this patent fact has not yet been made evident in official statistics. It is with the ordinary village weaver, who makes the common *dhoṭi*, *sāri*, or *puggaree* for the mass of the Indian population that I am now chiefly concerned, though some of the most valuable mechanical improvements, made centuries ago in Europe, which can be introduced into Indian hand-weaving, apply to the whole industry.

But before we can discuss mechanical improvements it is necessary to consider the present condition of the poor Indian village weaver. I saw a good deal of it in the course of six years' official touring through remote districts in the Madras Presidency, so I know how hopeless it seems to be, and must always seem, to the Anglo-Indian official. It is indeed a case which demands endless patience, tact, and sympathy; and I fully admit that often it is almost beyond the power of the best official methods to deal with it effectively. The hardworked Anglo-Indian officer, even the most sympathetic and devoted, cannot give the time and attention necessary to uplift such a mass of helpless and hopeless ignorance, apathy and despair. I know that in some districts of Madras the poorest weavers working from morn till night can barely earn the means to keep body and soul together, in the best of times.

When times begin to be bad they have the choice of crawling to the famine camp or dying of starvation. It is useless to talk to such helpless creatures of the wonders labour-saving appliances can do for them—to tell them that they might weave four cloths in the time they now weave one. At the beginning, all possible improvements they could make use of must be brought to their doors, given to them free of cost, and the time they take to learn the use of them must be paid for. Even this work a Government official could hardly undertake; he would be suspected of some deep, sinister motive. When I myself came to such weavers' huts I was generally mistaken for an officer of the Salt Department making secret enquiries into illicit manufacture.

Undoubtedly this lower stratum of the industrial population can be reached more effectively by private than by official agencies. It is here that the influence of the Indian home, striving after Indian domestic ideals, can be most effectively used. Indian women of the higher classes who learn weaving and spinning as a domestic industry, not for adding to their income, but for the psychological benefit of handicraft in the home, could, if they would, throw away the prejudices of caste pollution and extend sympathetic help to the village weaver toiling for bare subsistence. Indian young men who have practised weaving as a school or college exercise according to the curriculum I have suggested, could do the same. There is an immense field of usefulness for the 'Servants of India' trained in Mr. Gokhale's School, and for the 'Sons of India' enrolled by Mrs. Besant.

But do not let it be supposed that the mechanical improvements necessary for the continued existence of India's greatest industry are mainly a matter for expert knowledge. They are a few simple things, which any intelligent school boy or girl could learn to manipulate in a week, though they are so important for the village weaver that, were the Education Department as efficient as it should be, every village schoolmaster would teach them and every Inspector of Schools would be able to demonstrate them. Possibly some day a Director of Public Instruction may come to realise this, but having vainly hammered at official doors for many years I cannot waste much more time there. It is, after all, more important that India should learn the lesson of self-help.

These suggestions apply to the village weaver who is too poor, helpless, and ignorant to make any attempt to adopt even the simplest improvements to his apparatus. The educational measures hitherto employed, officially and unofficially, hardly touch his case at all. It is useless to provide schools, exhibitions and demonstrations of improved appliances for his edification. He cannot afford to leave his loom to attend them and has not the means, even if he had the energy, to obtain the required improvements which might help him out of his difficulties; though the cost of them would seem to be a small matter, for a total expenditure of ten or twelve rupees would provide him with apparatus which would certainly double, and, in some cases, treble his out-put.

In most European countries, if there were such a clear case for making a vast improvement in a great national industry, there would be sufficient public spirit to create at once a powerful national organisation to provide the money and means of instruction required for the purpose, even if Government assistance were not forthcoming. In India, this kind of public spirit is at present mainly restricted to political activities, and Indian political leaders do not yet seem to realise how much stronger their position would be if they devoted their attention to constructive work, rather than to political manœuvres, such as the boycott of European manufactures, which can only be carried out by inflaming the animosities of the masses—a very dangerous game for all parties.

India requires somewhat less of the keen-witted political lawyer, and a great deal more of the level-headed organiser and man of business, to help to solve her artistic and industrial problems. If Bengali politicians had used the funds they collected for their propaganda in financing model weaving villages in fifty suitable centres in Bengal they would have done a great deal more than the boycott has done to put the Swaḍeshi movement on a sound economic footing. Now that the Serampore Weaving College has started work nothing would be easier than to organise such model weaving villages in different parts of India, under the charge of the trained teachers and managers which the College could supply. The capital required for fifty model villages would be much less than is necessary for launching one sham Swaḍeshi power-loom mill, and there is not the least doubt that with good management they could become self-supporting and profitable in a very short time. The proof of this is that *even without any improved apparatus* the village industry in favourable localities can be resuscitated and made comparatively flourishing. I have several times called public attention to the success which Mr. A. F. Maconochie, I. C. S. had, while he was Collector of Sholapur in the Bombay Presidency, in reviving the local weaving industry by the simple expedient of making arrangements to provide the weavers with raw materials on reasonable terms, advancing them cash at reasonable rates in the slack season, and enabling them to obtain the best market price for their labour—all of which advantages are denied them by the rapacious village money-lender. In three years the condition of three hundred weavers had greatly improved, twenty-five of them had paid off all their old debts, and recovered their mortgaged property from the *sowcars*; and at the same time the scheme itself had given a fair dividend on the capital used.

If this can be done without any attempt to improve the methods and appliances of the weavers, it stands to reason that an efficient organisation which gives both financial and practical educational assistance would be certain of success. The example of ten thousand weavers in the Serampore District of Bengal is a proof that simple improved appliances can enable village weavers to double their earnings even without any outside assistance.

I will indicate roughly how the scheme might be worked. It should be understood, that, though good management would undoubtedly secure a fair return on the capital invested, the first object of the scheme should not be to secure dividends for the middle class investor, but to put a great national industry upon a sound economic basis—an object which should surely commend itself to the whole-hearted support of every Swaḍeshi reformer. I would fix the initial capital at one lakh of rupees, a sum amply sufficient to finance fifty model weaving villages with an average of one hundred weavers each, but it could equally well be started with half a lakh of rupees and twenty-five villages. The scheme should be managed by a Committee or Board of Directors, located at a suitable centre, where a deposit for the yarn, dyes, and all other raw materials of good quality required by the weavers should be established. In charge of each of the fifty or twenty-five local branches—the weaving villages—there should be a trained manager capable of instructing the weavers in the use of the fly-shuttle and other simple mechanical improvements such as those now used in Serampore. To win the confidence of the weavers should be the local manager's first endeavour. At first he should limit himself to working on the lines of Mr. Maconochie's scheme, retailing to the weavers at a small profit the materials supplied from the central depôt, advancing cash on the security of finished cloths to help them over the slack season, and assisting them to dispose of their cloths in the best markets, etc. Gradually he should show the most intelligent of the weavers the use of simple labour-saving appliances and supply them free of cost, only taking in return, after three months' trial, a fair percentage of the increased out-put which they were enabled to make by the use of them. Some of the Members of the Central Board, or Inspectors appointed by them, would have to visit the local centres from time to time to satisfy themselves of the conduct of the local managers.

I believe that in less than three years under a scheme of this kind, the first fifty or twenty-five model weaving villages would need little further assistance. The best weavers, at least, would be released from the clutches of the local *sowcars*, and would have realised the advantages of simple labour-saving appliances. The Directors of the scheme could then, of course, devote their attention to other centres. With men of good business capacity and power of organisation at the head of it, this scheme would do more for India in five years than all the Technical Schools have done in fifty. India does not require to create the technical skill for her great weaving industry; the skill is already created. It is only recklessly wasted for want of proper organisation.

I have dealt with the lower stratum of the weaving populations consisting of the ordinary village weavers who are too poor and too miserable to make ordinary educational methods applicable to their case; but there still remain a great many of the more intelligent and skilful weavers who could and would profit greatly by suitable object-lessons placed before them.

In this case much depends upon the character of the object-lesson chosen for their instruction. Ordinary exhibitions and demonstrations of weaving appliances, however useful they may be for small capitalists of the middle class, are not as a rule very convincing for the practical weaver; at all events, he rarely has enterprise enough to venture upon altering his usual methods on the strength of such object-lessons as these. The best and most convincing object-lesson which has yet been put before the weavers of India, undoubtedly, was the hand-loom factory which was started seventy or eighty years ago at Serampore when that place was under the Danish

Government. Of the exact history of that hand-loom factory I have not been able to discover much. How long it existed, and what the promoters gained by it, are matters of small importance. What really matters is, first, that ten thousand village weavers profited so largely by the lessons it taught them, that their earnings are now double those of similar weavers who have not had such lessons; secondly that they have maintained their individual existence as village craftsmen, and are much less indebted to the *sowcars* than the ordinary weaver; and, thirdly, that the factory itself has been absorbed by the village industry.

Now you have in Madras a very able and energetic exponent of European commercialism. Mr. Alfred Chatterton, Director of Technical Enquiries, who holds views on technical education directly opposed to mine, though in the matter of hand-loom weaving I can claim him as a partial and somewhat unwilling convert to my propaganda. He has repeatedly told you that the only hope for the hand-loom weaver is to commercialise his industry, through the European factory system, and to quote his own words, that "to attempt to assist the artisans of India and to neglect the results of the mercantile efforts of the whole of the last century (in Europe) is to court failure". To him the factory is the ideal to be aimed at, the *summum bonum* and the indispensable thing in all industry, artistic or otherwise—for to Mr. Chatterton the artistic factor does not count for much. He has warned you against the 'sentimentalism' and 'dilettantism' of the artist. Indian art must submit to be dragged behind the car of human 'progress,' which, in his view, means the progress of mechanical invention.

In my view, the factory in hand-loom weaving may be useful as a means to an end—the education of the village weaver—but it is neither an indispensable nor a desirable thing in itself. In the hand-weaving industry all the economic advantages of the factory system can be obtained by the village weaver through intelligent co-operation and organisation, as Sir F. W. Nicholson maintained in an able paper he contributed to the *Madras Mail* in December 1901. I do not ignore the results of the mercantile efforts of the whole of the last century in Europe as Mr. Chatterton would make you believe. It is really Mr. Chatterton who is greatly behind the times in his policy, as Sir F. C. Nicholson showed in his paper. He said:

In the latter half, chiefly indeed, in the last quarter of the last century, a new factor has come into industrial life, *viz.*, the principle of co-operation, organisation for the purchase of raw material, implements, etc., for the sale of manufactured goods, and for the necessary credit; and it is in this new factor that the hand-loom weavers will find the power of competing with the large mill-owner and the dealer. The old Guilds and Town Leagues of the West can never be revived, but the new co-operation by mutual contract will be a permanent feature of the new century. Already the accounts of the new powers and hopes which it creates are almost beyond belief. In many Societies it has effected a saving to producers of almost half the costs, while it has largely increased their effective receipts. There seems no limit to the economies to be effected, to the material good to be obtained, to the qualities of character that may be evolved . . . It is not strange when the character of co-operation is considered, that the characters of the individual workers are developed by such co-operation; foresight, industriousness, punctuality, honesty, business-capacity, and the other characteristics of a thriving, hopeful and self-respecting community become the rule and not the exception.

The co-operative system, also, by preserving the individuality of the craftsman is also the best guarantee for the preservation of the artistic element in Indian hand-loom weaving. I do not, like Mr. Chatterton, regard this as a subordinate consideration, but as the most vital of all. To preserve Indian art is to preserve India. The really vital point in the object-lesson of Serampore is that Indian craftsmanship has survived, and the factory system has been eliminated or absorbed, by the traditional organisation of village handicraft. The principle of co-operation will do even more for that organisation than the factory system can ever do.

Accepting the factory system as one of the means but not the only means or the most desirable means, for helping the village weaver to help himself, I will now explain what I have done to promote the system of hand-loom factories for small capitalists in India. In October 1904, I addressed a letter to the London *Times* inviting the co-operation of the best European makers of textile machinery in the task of improving the hand-apparatus now used by Indian weavers. I also addressed personally many such firms in America. The only response I received was from one of the best English firms, Messrs. George Hattersley & Sons, Ltd., of Keightley, who some years previously had been asked by the Roumanian Government to produce a loom suitable for the hand industry in that State. The hand-apparatus which they invented for this purpose was the means of promoting a very great revival of hand-weaving in the Balkan States. Messrs. Hattersley have introduced about twelve thousand improved looms into that part of Europe, the Roumanian Government allowing them to be imported free of duty. The result has been that the local hand-weaving industry has been successful in keeping power-loom productions almost entirely out of the local markets.

Messrs. Hattersley then began under my advice to produce apparatus suitable for India. They sent an expert to India to study local conditions and have spent considerable capital in perfecting all kinds of apparatus especially adapted for Indian hand loom factories. With their expert knowledge of all the latest developments of textile machinery in Europe they have attacked all the most difficult technical problems connected with the Indian industry, from the winding and sizing of the yarn until the cloth is taken from the loom, and no one in Europe or in India has brought so much scientific knowledge to bear upon these questions.

Last year at the Franco-British Exhibition I arranged with the India Office that they should have a special exhibit in the Indian section, for which the highest award for hand-power machinery, a gold medal, was given by the expert judges. They are now exporting to India every week sufficient improved loom and preparatory apparatus for a small hand factory, not a very great result from a mercantile point of view, but for the development of the Indian industry and for the education of the village weaver it is of the highest significance. One hand factory, only seventy or eighty years ago in Bengal, was the means of enabling ten thousand village weavers to learn improved mechanical processes and to double their earnings. Now, through Messrs. Hattersley's instrumentality alone, India receives *every week* material for one hand factory—material which, through the principle of co-operation, could also be used in the model weaving villages I have advocated.

In a recent letter, Messrs. Hattersley informed me that they believe they have now overcome the difficulty of beaming and sizing warps by hand, with their latest hand-power, beaming and slasher-sizing machines, designed for an out-put of about fifty hand-looms.

These are two of the most difficult technical problems connected with Indian hand-weaving. The beaming machine is for putting yarn on to the warper's beams direct from the warping bobbins by hand; and the sizing machine is for sizing the yarn as it passes from the warper's beams on to the loom beam. The great difficulty of drying the yarn after sizing it is overcome by forcing hot air through four layers of warp by means of a fan worked by a hand-wheel. Besides various kinds of improved looms, worked by hand or by foot, adapted for weaving silk, cotton, linen or wool for *sāris* and *ḍhoṭis*, etc., as well as for small wares such as lamp wicks and working four or five times as fast as the ordinary village loom, Messrs. Hattersley have produced a simple and excellent warping mill and creel, weft winder, warping bobbin-winder, pirn winder, etc. Among their latest inventions is a hand-loom for heavy fabrics such as dhurries and reed sun-blinds, together with the necessary preparatory apparatus.

Though Mr. Chatterton has condemned off-hand Messrs. Hattersley's looms as being too heavy and complicated for the Indian weaver, the fact remains that they have been already successfully used in a hand-factory in Ganjam, and in many other places. They have been fitted up and repaired by an ordinary village blacksmith and worked by an ordinary village weaver. As a weaving expert, Mr. Chatterton has no claim to ask the public to put his experience by the side of the best technical skill of Europe, for his experience in the matter only began when I drew his attention to the question, and though he has superciliously alluded to my efforts as the 'dilettantism of the artist,' I prefer to rely upon the best technical skill of Europe in these questions, rather than upon the amateur experiments of departmental officials. I have no interest whatever in recommending Messrs. Hattersley, beyond my knowledge of their position as the best English technical experts, and as the only ones who have ventured a considerable amount of capital in perfecting weaving apparatus for India—so far without any adequate return. The Roumanian Government aided them considerably in making a success of their apparatus in that State, and I think that in their efforts to perfect the mechanical efficiency of weaving appliances in India they are entitled to more encouragement than they have received from the official who is responsible for these matters in Madras.

CHAPTER XIII

INDUSTRIAL REFORM IN EUROPE

I HAVE before drawn attention to the significant fact that while many experts and empirics are continually advising India to exchange her old lamps for new ones, and persuading Indian youths to go to Europe to learn methods of art and industry, the attention of industrial reformers in Europe is becoming more and more concentrated on the very methods and principles in art and in industry which India is being urged to discard.

There has been recently a considerable discussion in the London Press on a declaration of the new Lord Mayor, that he intended to work for the revival of the apprenticeship system. Lord Avebury has a scheme for adapting this system to modern industrial conditions, and conferences on the subject will be shortly initiated at an opening meeting to be held at the Mansion House. The result of these deliberations should be of the greatest value to all who are interested in industrial reform in India, and possibly the fact that London English technical experts and city merchants are taking an interest in such matters may have some influence on the official policy in India.

The apprenticeship system is the foundation of the whole indigenous industrial system in India, as it was formerly in Europe, though, up to the present, all official schemes have entirely ignored it and tried to supersede it by factories and by technical schools on the European model.

Mr. A. J. Penty, a well-known architect and advocate of the restoration of the Guild System (which is the European counterpart of the Indian caste industrial system), in an interview on the subject, with regard to technical schools, said :

> They are no substitute at all for apprenticeship. Boys all learning together in a class do not pass on in a rational way from stage to stage: they learn *en masse* and so there is no real individual growth. Of course schools can help in a theoretical way, but there is no substitute for the sound practical training given by apprenticeship.

Small workshops (such as the Indian caste system creates) and not more factories, were, he said, needed in the European industrial system. All the best work that comes to England from Paris is done in small workshops. "Paris," says one economist, "is a beehive of small workshops," and Mr. Penty was convinced that any movement for the revival of the apprenticeship system that does not emphasise the importance of reviving crafts—not merely as a commercial, but as artistic concerns—is doomed to failure. But in the present state of unemployment when the skilled trades are so terribly over-crowded, it is useless to increase the number of skilled workmen without increasing the demand for their work. It was the demand for artistic things which created the necessity for the small workshops and brought back the handicraftsmen. Mr. Penty had no doubt that the unemployment problem was connected with the absence of artistic demand. Many of the ancient Greek temples were relief works, built to afford a temporary solution for the unemployment problem; and that was one of the grounds on which Pericles justified their erection.

The conditions in India are precisely similar; only there is no lack of skilled handicraftsmen. They exist in large numbers already. Industrial empirics in India pretend to solve the unemployment problem by methods which have produced unemployment in Europe. Unemployment is created in India, as in Europe, by the want of artistic demand. In India, as in Europe, the lack of artistic demand is very largely the result of a bad educational system. There would be a great opening for Pericles' expedient in India if the Public Works Department were conducted on sound artistic principles.

Industry, as Mr. Penty observed, needs some motive force other than pure commercial gain, and not until it can get it will it be able to grapple successfully with its attendant evils; and this impulse is the artistic impulse. In a recent report the United States Consul in Paris says:

France is industrially prosperous because she commands the rarest and surest of assets—the æsthetic taste which creates models and standards for other peoples, and the consummate handicraft which multiplies, in the product, ten, twenty, or a hundred times the value of the material of which it is composed. It is this which enables French ateliers and workshops to turn out the choice products which defy the tariff walls of other nations and makes Paris a Mecca, not only for a vast multitude of cultivated amateurs, but also for merchants from foreign countries who deal in the choicest and most valuable forms of merchandise.

With these progressive views of European industrial experts may be contrasted those of Mr. A. C. Chatterjee, B.A., I.C.S., in industrial matters a disciple of Mr. Chatterton, who in a paper on 'The Needs and Methods of Industrial development in India,' read before the East India Association, hardly alluded to the Indian apprenticeship and guild systems of handicraft except in terms of depreciation, and argued that the factory system which produces unemployment in Europe was desirable in India, because the use of complex machinery "enhances by a considerable degree the demand for judgment, intelligence and general faculties of a high order".

It is necessary to explain that the question which he considered of the greatest importance was "whether the wealth of India is increasing as fast as the wealth of other countries of the world". Mr. Chatterjee is raising a question which Europe began to consider for herself some centuries ago, but after some bitter experience we are now discovering that there are other more important things to think of. We are beginning to find that the old lamps which we exchanged so hastily were more valuable than we thought them. Let us hope that India will not be so foolish as to part with hers.

I must here bring to a conclusion my suggestions on this all important subject. India now stands at the parting of the ways: it is for her leaders to say which they will choose. The one is to surrender all her past traditions, all her intellectual freedom, and in the blind lust for the commercial wealth and political power, which seems to dull imaginations and perverted intellects the highest object of human endeavour, to follow the ignoble crowd which has gone before down the same path, every man fighting for himself, struggling to catch up the vanguard, and hoping, sooner or later, amidst unspeakable filth, squalor and misery, to join in the reckless scramble for gold, such as is witnessed to-day in the great commercial cities of Europe and the so-called 'free' America. This path ends in the quagmire in which many great empires, and many great democracies which never learnt the true secret of self-government, have been swallowed up.

The other path is to keep steadfastly in the direction which India's own spiritual teachers have always pointed out, cherishing the great artistic traditions committed to your charge as a most sacred trust; and, if you must look to the West for more light and leading, to use the insight of spiritual intuition to discriminate between falsehood and truth, to know wisdom from ignorance.

India is not poor as your politicians would make you believe. India has riches which would make her first among all nations, only in their blindness her leaders do not see them or know how to use them. What the better sense of Europe is struggling to regain, India has in abundance ; what India really has lost is not political power nor material prosperity, but the spiritual vision which will enable her to realise her own wealth. When that is regained the lessons which she once taught Europe will come back to her mind and she will lead the world in art, science and industry as she has done before. When the mind of India is free, everything else will be achieved. "Seek first the kingdom of God and His righteousness and all things shall be added unto you."

I say again, if you look to Europe or America for teachers, take heed that you choose wisely. None but the ignorant or charlatans will recommend you the paths of western commercialism as leading to true national prosperity. Lord Morley said in the House of Lords, on a recent memorable occasion: "There is a great feeling prevailing in this country—quite beyond the lines of party—of pity, of sympathy and horror at the miseries which our industrial system entails." This is a true expression of the better feeling of Europe, which is above the selfish and narrow interests of individuals or of nations. Dr. Coomâraswâmy, than whom no one knows better what is true progress in the West, in his last publication, *The Message of the East*, says:

The western nations, after a period of unparalleled success in the investigation of the concrete world, the 'conquest of nature,' and the adaptation of mechanical contrivances to the material ends of life, are approaching in every department a certain critical period. The far-reaching developments of commercialism are undermining their own stability. One-tenth of the British population dies in the gaol, the workhouse or the lunatic asylum. The increasing contrast between extremes of wealth and poverty, the unemployed and many other urgent problems point the same moral. Extreme developments of vulgarity and selfishness imply the necessary reaction. In science, the limit of possible investigation by physical means is in sight. The main body of scientific men cannot much longer avoid the necessity for the investigation of super-physical phenomena by new methods. The problems of the new psychology have made an obsolete science of the old. In all the arts, the extreme development of the critical, scientific and observing faculties has almost extinguished creative power. Science has corrupted art, until the aims of both are confused. . . . .

There is already abundant evidence of that permeation of western thought by Indian Philosophy which Schopenhauer so clearly foresaw. The East has indeed revealed a new world to the West, which will be the inspiration of a 'Renaissance,' more profound and far-reaching than that which resulted from the re-discovery of the classic world of the West. It is the irony of fate that while the outward and visible Anglicisation of the East is only too apparent, this inward and subtle Indianisation of the West has, as it were, stolen a march in the night, and already there are groups of western thinkers whose purposes and principles are more truly Indian than are those of the average English-educated Indian of to-day. The West can no longer afford to ignore the wisdom of the East in any single department of culture.

This Indianisation of western thought is the most interesting phenomenon in the modern world. The difference between it and the Anglicisation of the East is that it is clearly leading to a true renaissance, whereas most Indians of the present generation who have assimilated the learning of modern Europe, for material advantages, have thrown away, intellectually and spiritually, more than they have gained.

Nevertheless I am optimistic enough to believe that this process of Anglicisation, in spite of its present disadvantages, will eventually lead to a similar intellectual and spiritual renaissance in the East. For though the crowd seems at present to be pressing down the other path—as the foolish always follow fools—there is yet a small band of pioneers with steadfast purpose and clearer insight, seeking the way of true progress and freedom—the way along which the best and wisest men of East and West have always joined and always will join together in comradeship for the common good of humanity.